LOVING THE LOST

Loving the Lost

The Principles and Practice of Cell Church

LAURENCE SINGLEHURST

KINGSWAY PUBLICATIONS
EASTBOURNE

First published 2001

Unless otherwise indicated, biblical quotations are
from the New International Version © 1973, 1978, 1984
by the International Bible Society.

ISBN 0 85476 753 3

*Names of individuals have been changed
in this book in order to protect identities.*

Published by
KINGSWAY PUBLICATIONS
Lottbridge Drove, Eastbourne, BN23 6NT, England.
Email: books@kingsway.co.uk

Book design and production for the publishers by
Bookprint Creative Services, P.O. Box 827, BN21 3YJ, England.
Printed in Great Britain.

Contents

Acknowledgements

I am very aware that this book could not have been written without my involvement in the River Church, where I first encountered the essence of cell and celebration. So I want to thank them for years of fellowship and support.

But in particular, this book owes a tremendous amount to Ralph Neighbour and Bill Beckham, who have been my spiritual parents in this particular journey. So I acknowledge wholeheartedly their pioneer thinking and example, and see myself as someone trying to make these wonderful ideas practical and easily accessible.

I also want to thank my friend Ila Howard, who has typed this manuscript and listened to me for many hours in that process. And also Liz West who is a fellow pioneer within the cell church movement in the UK, who wrote many of the summaries of the chapters, gave invaluable guidance and co-authored with me the Moving to Cells appendix at the back of the book.

Lastly, a special thanks as always to my wonderful wife, Ailish, and my three special children, Kiera, Justyn and Laura.

Foreword

In the refrain of a first-century chorus (Ephesians 5:14), Paul passionately admonishes the church about holy living that leads to the conversion of the lost:

> Wake up, O sleeper,
> rise from the dead,
> and Christ will shine on you.

The church has gradually begun to stir from its spritual slumber induced by institutional religion, academic intellectualism and twentieth-century secularism. A series of movements over the past two decades gives hope that the long hibernation of the church is coming to an end. Healthy spiritual movements are born out of biblical theology, nurtured in revelation vision and applied through practical methodology. Among recent movements the cell church uniquely provides a practical design for the church to actually mobilize every member for ministry and evangelism.

Loving the Lost is written from a cell church perspective and is part of God's wake-up call for the church in the twenty-first century. Laurence Singlehurst has personally experienced the theology and vision of New Testament community life. And God has also used him to test out practical methods for living out the theology and vision that is ultimately demonstrated in witness and evangelism. This is a practical 'how to' book, with a major focus on how the church is to love the lost through New Testament community.

The book builds up to practical suggestions in Appendix 3, 'Moving to Cells'. This supplies the basic principles and practices of cell church and then walks a pastor through the process of starting a prototype cell that can be a model for transition to an operating cell church.

William A. Beckham

1

What Is Church?

Obeying the commands of Christ

If you were to ask a hundred people, 'What is church?' you would probably get a hundred different answers. And if you were to ask, 'What is the church called to do?' the answers would number in their thousands. It seems to me, however, that the answer could be summed up with one simple statement: 'The church is called to obey the commands of Christ.'

Here's another question: 'Why bother with cell churches?' To answer that, we need to look more closely at the first two questions, and then perhaps we will see how the model of cell church can help us.

In Mark 12 Jesus told his disciples that they were to do two things. First: 'Love the Lord your God with all your heart and with all your soul and with all your mind and with all your strength' (v. 30). Second: '"Love your neighbour as yourself." There is no other commandment greater than these' (v. 31). In addition, the New Testament church was living in the echo of

Jesus' Great Commission: 'Go into all the world and preach the good news to all creation' (Mark 16:15). So the church was, and still is, called to do three things: love God, love one another, and love the lost.

These commands are not just sterile commands – they represent God's vision for the world. His hope has always been that the world will be filled with love. However, if we as humans are going to love, we must first lay down our lives for a concept that is bigger than ourselves, for as long as we have self at the centre, we will have problems.

Loving God

In loving God, we are not satisfying his ego or trying to make him feel good – he doesn't *need* our love in that sense. In loving God, we are recognizing that here is someone who is far more valuable, wonderful and awesome than ourselves. In laying down our lives for a greater cause, we are set free to love one another and reach out from our own communities into the world. This has always been God's vision, and it is what the church has been commanded to do.

So if church is about loving God, loving one another, loving the lost and providing a structure and the means to do this, the idea of cell church must reflect and make real these primary ideas. If we look at the early church in the very first days of the book of Acts, we see that as the disciples sought to obey the commands of Christ, they seemed to model church in two distinct ways. First, the book of Acts shows us that they met in each other's houses: they ate together; they encouraged one another; they looked out for one another, and out of caring relationships many people were won into the kingdom of God. The early church was a loose, organic structure, and these groups formed its basic infrastructure. Yet in the book of Acts, we see another structure. Even in the very early days of the church, people still met in the Temple. In the bigger gathering there was teaching, encouraging and worship, and both Peter and Paul recognized that this was church as well.

Church historians tell us that up until the third century, the church was often living in times of persecution, particularly in parts of the world under Roman influence. Families were living in what would look to us like tenement blocks of flats. There would be quite a number of households in these flats, with maybe a particular family having two or three rooms, and husband, wife, grandparents, uncles and cousins all living together. As these people converted to Christianity, they would have church in their houses.

Sometimes local bishops might have gathered together these house churches to meet for teaching and worship in secret places, but although there were those who were leaders and apostles, there was a tremendous sense that ministry was not done by the special few, but by the whole body of Christ. One of the secrets of the early church was not just the structure of big and small, celebration and cell, but also that these structures empowered every individual with a sense of purpose and destiny.

However, in the fourth century there was a major change. Up until then, the house churches would have held at most 50 people. But the conversion to Christianity of Emperor Constantine at the beginning of the fourth century meant that the church no longer needed to be underground. As Christianity was now officially recognized, believers were able to build bigger buildings. These buildings inevitably became the centre of worship and the whole dynamic of church changed. Slowly but surely church became the larger congregational unit. This set a pattern that has remained until modern times, not only in terms of structure, but also in terms of ministry. From the fourth century, ministry was increasingly seen to be done by the special few people who were called and appointed.

Throughout church history there have been a few movements that broke away from this pattern and saw church again as both the small and the big – the Moravians and the Methodists, to name just two. These movements not only created new and radical structures in terms of cell and celebration, they also brought the concept of the body of Christ back to the forefront. Leaders were there to equip the body for the work of ministry, to enable individuals to obey the commands of Christ, particularly within the Methodist structure. Thus began the non-conformist movement, which changed the course of British history between 1730 and 1870.

Even radical new movements, like the charismatic movement, began with a real sense of wanting the church to be both small and big and desiring to see every member involved in ministry. In the end, though, many became conformed to the historical pattern – the congregation became the main unit of church again, and, largely speaking, ministry was seen to be done by the paid professionals. We need to ask ourselves, 'Do these big meetings really equip and enable the church to obey the commands of Christ in terms of loving one another, loving God and loving the lost?' If we are honest, we would probably have to answer, 'Not very well.' It is true to say that in the big meeting we can love God by worshipping as a corporate company, we can be taught and encouraged through the Scriptures, and we can sense the awesomeness of God through the use of ceremony and symbol. But there are other aspects of our love of God that the big meeting cannot deal with. In a big meeting, it is hard to have personal accountability. It is easy for our love for God to become a sterile religious thing, rather than something that is active and vibrant.

Perhaps the truth is that if any of us are really going to love God, we need the help that accountability gives us. This is the challenge of fellow Christians who ask awkward questions, who lovingly seek to confront us with the inconsistency of our lives, who challenge us with the words of James that faith without works is dead, who show us that if our worship of God does not change us and make us better people it is perhaps just a form and not a reality. Particularly in our modern world, where there are so many distractions, so many things that use up our energy and time, we need more than ever some honest, open, accountable Christianity. This can only properly take place in small groups, where people meet together in a cell and hold one another accountable for their love of God.

We see this model in the early Methodist movement, where in their equivalent of a cell they asked themselves three questions: 'What temptations have you faced in the last week?', 'What sins have you committed in the last week?', and maybe best of all, 'What means of grace is God opening up to you?' In other words, this is not a strong leader dishing out heavy accountability – this is members of the body of Christ helping each other to have a living love for God. No wonder these radical non-conformists changed our society – they started a revival that lasted, in the view of some historians, from 1730 to 1870.

Loving each other

God's second command to the church is to love one another, but can we really love each other when viewing the backs of heads in Sunday congregations? Is this structure really helping us to care for the church? It's probably better than no structure at all, but the reality for most of us is that in the big group we're lost, we're not quite sure what our responsibilities are, and we perhaps rely on a few professional church people to do the loving and caring for us. This is OK as far as it goes, but it falls a long way short of being the body of Christ. God's dream is that each of us is an active member of a Christian community – that each one of us has our part to play in caring for other Christians.

In a cell where we have about ten to fifteen people, we will soon become very aware of each other's strengths and weaknesses, practical needs and concerns. Here is an opportunity for us to obey the commands of Christ and love one another: if someone is out of work, we can give money; if someone is sick, we can visit and cook their food; if someone is discouraged, we can listen and pray. If we think about our postmodern society, what does the world out there expect church to be like? What are people looking for that shows them Christianity is genuine and practical? We need go no further than the words of Jesus: 'By this all men will know that you are my disciples, if you love one another' (John 13:35).

In other words, in our fragmented society, people are genuinely looking for community. There is a hunger for relationships: the more rigid and isolated our society becomes, the greater the opportunity for the church to demonstrate something radical and different.

If our communities and towns are scattered with cells of people who are actively and lovingly caring for one another in tangible ways that can be clearly seen, and if these little communities are actively seeking to share this love in an outward dynamic, perhaps we will have an evangelistic tool of real power. We will be showing the authenticity of the Christian message, of the body of Christ. We will be answering that human ache that occurs as our society becomes more and more fragmented, leading to isolation, whereby people are desperately wanting to belong to a little tribe or community. We can demonstrate through our lives what it really means to love one another.

So we have seen that we can love God in a big meeting to a certain extent, and we can have a glimmer of community, but in a cell or a smaller group you get fully fledged reality.

Loving the lost

We now come to the last thing the church is called to do – loving the lost. Here most powerfully we see the limitations of the big meeting. First, it would seem that in the radical church Jesus is asking every church member to love the lost. How do we go about this in our congregational model of church? We employ an evangelist and delegate some of our responsibilities to him. We hope the lost will be convinced by hearing the message. In reality, not many non-believers are ready to attend these meetings and respond to the message. So I am not saying that it is a bad thing to have an evangelist, but in the end we have to face the reality that we must individually obey the commands of Christ and reach out to our neighbours.

Another limit of the big meeting is that we can lecture people and tell them how to live a Christ-like life, but we have no idea whether they are really doing it. As all speakers and teachers will know, however dynamic a communicator you are, particularly in our modern world, the impact of what you say in the big meeting is very quickly lost. A preacher who recently said that he wasn't sure how long people remembered what he was telling them, wasn't surprised when one bright spark put his hand up and said, 'What did you just say?' If we want to love the lost and demonstrate that love, we have to give people the confidence to get out of their Christian ghettos. We want to hold people accountable to obey Christ, and this is impossible in a big meeting. But in a cell, where we are all on the same level, we have a unique opportunity to help one another find ways to share our faith, to encourage one another when we're frustrated, to keep evangelism and sharing our faith and touching our world, not as an agenda item that comes up on the church calendar once or twice a year, but as our weekly and monthly passion. We will individually and corporately obey the commands of Christ, and we will find ways to encourage each other to keep on reaching out and demonstrating the love of Christ.

Why cell church?

In this first chapter we have seen that if the church is about obeying the commands of Christ, we cannot obey them properly with church existing as only the big meeting. We need a new definition of church – a big meeting for the place of celebration, but also the cell, where we mutually support and encourage one another to do what God has called us to do.

Summary

- As 'church' our mandate is: love God, love one another and love the lost.
- The early church structure included small gatherings of real community and large meetings for teaching and worship.

- The changes in the third century took the church into congregational meetings run by 'professionals' and largely lost the dynamic of the small meeting where all could play their part.
- In order to obey the commands of Christ there needs to be accountable relationships, worked out in small groups of honest relationships.

2

The Definition of Cell Church

Having seen that church is about obeying the commands of Christ, and that cells enable us to do this more easily, we might ask the question, 'What's the difference between cell church and any normal church with small groups?' In simple terms the difference is this: cell churches have a very clearly defined set of beliefs, values and structures, which in the end draws some radical conclusions. (We will explore these beliefs, values and structures in the forthcoming chapters.) The cell church proposes that cell is church, and that caring discipleship and evangelism, and as many of the functions of church as possible, will be carried out in the life of the cell. If caring discipleship and evangelism is done in the cell, it means that the cells cannot just be interest groups. Meeting together just for evangelism is not sufficient. Meeting together just to be blessed or taught is also not sufficient. Meeting around any interest is not sufficient. That is not to say that these are bad things to do, but this is not the concept of cell church.

The cell church really does want to provide the basic concepts of caring and discipling. The cell will be the place of primary spiritual growth, of teaching and of Christians looking after one another. It will also be the place that takes the primary responsibility for evangelism for the church, in as much as this is the place where individuals are empowered and held accountable for reaching out to their own network of friends and contacts.

The cell church believes that the big meetings are still part of church and are church as well, but they are there to serve the life of the cells. In the big meetings, you will get a dynamic of corporate worship, teaching and leadership that may not be manifested elsewhere. The cell church sees that the cell is the primary building block of church. Therefore, all other structures need to serve the cells and not be set up in such a way that they pull people away from their commitment to the cells.

This of course does not mean that churches shouldn't have structures (in a later chapter, we will look at some of the structures a cell church might have), but they are there to serve and empower the cells and not be in competition with them. The cell church would want to come to the ultimate position where to be a member of the church you would need to be a member of a cell. This is because cell is the primary building block, and if you are going to be pastored and cared for, if you are going to participate in the life of the church and develop your ministry and gifts, there is no other place to be than in the cell.

What is a cell church?

Here is a simple definition of what makes a cell church:

• church as cell and celebration, with the cell being the building block;

- every member in ministry, which means every individual in the body has a role and part to play in God's purposes;
- each cell member taking a responsibility to have a network of unchurched friends they are reaching out to and seeking to evangelize;
- a sense of mutual accountability to obey the commands of Christ – to love God, love one another and love the lost;
- empowering people and encouraging them into a sense of destiny and purpose in what they do on a Monday to Friday basis.

These are just some of the things that make a cell church different in terms of its beliefs, structures and values. But be warned: if we don't understand these beliefs and the dynamic values we've drawn from them, we will only create a new legalistic container and will be robbed of the important things that God is trying to do at this time and the huge potential of this way of being church.

In terms of beliefs, there are perhaps two things we might want to add. One has to do with how we understand church: the small group in the early New Testament *was* church – it was not additional to church. This small group discipled, cared for and empowered people for evangelism; it was a place where responsibility was taken for disciplining the new converts, and it multiplied.

It is essential that we cross this divide in our thinking. If we really believe this, it will alter our values and our structures. Cells will not just get a fraction of church leaders' attention; they will get the majority. Cell leaders will be the most trained and cared for people in the system. It will also affect the finances of the church. If we really believe cell is church, we will be putting our financial resources into it, and will provide for the training and equipping of the cell leaders. This might mean that some asp of church life won't receive as many resources as historically they might have done, but this is part of the radical shift. As mentioned earlier, we must not underestimate how significant a shift this is and why it is so important to our thinking.

We have a very good example in the house church movement in the United Kingdom where small groups of people started meeting in houses, and this was the building block of church. However, this belief was not clear enough in people's minds, and over a period of years the power of the historical model of church slowly won out. Thirty years later, the congregation within the 'house' or 'new church' movement has become the building block of church, and the small groups have, in most cases, been relegated to the side lines. As a result of this, the small group leaders have not been trained or encouraged, and there is no clear dynamic in terms of values and structures. There are now signs that some of the new churches are awake to this and are moving towards a cell-based structure. So this simple belief that church is both the small and the big, the cell and the celebration, is crucial to the understanding of the cell idea.

A second thing we need to get our heads round is the fact that the New Testament teaches that every member of the body of Christ has a ministry, which they should play out in the context of local church, the community and their home and family. Even in the relatively new charismatic movement, where there was an emphasis on every member in ministry, we have often fallen back on the familiar habits of full-time Christian workers being the ones with ministry. The result of this understanding is that everybody else feels slightly insignificant or that Christian ministry is not for them. Another danger that creeps in is that we develop a consumer mindset, and church becomes about only receiving.

If we really believe that every member has a part to play in ministry, this belief will impact our values and radically change our structures. We will have cell leaders who are committed to facilitation, so that every cell member has an important contribution to make in the cell. We will have church leaders who will empower and develop cell leaders, and give space for their people to manifest and develop the gifts that God has given them.

The heroes of the modern church have been the well-known Christian leaders – those full-time workers who have done great and wonderful things for God. We can be thankful to God for these people, but in the new millennium we need to see a new type of hero. This new hero is the average, ordinary cell member doing what God has called them to do. They will feel empowered and encouraged in the context of their church life, in whatever they do from Monday to Friday, and in the context of their families. They will be the nation changers.

Christian ministry will be something that relates to the whole of an individual's life, in terms of church, family and the local community, as well as in their daily work.

A Christian leader spoke to a group of business people at Spring Harvest. He asked how many of them had heard a message from the pulpit that told them that what they did from Monday to Friday could and should be ministry and was extremely important in the purposes of God, that what they were doing was being 'salt and light' in the workplace, and that they were fulfilling the command to Christians to change the environment and impact the structures of society. Sad to relate, out of a group of about 300 at Spring Harvest, two people put up their hands. Can you see how important it is to re-emphasize every member in ministry?

Here's another example. A company director, who was a committed Christian, drove to his office every day listening to spiritual music and inspirational teaching tapes. He parked his car in the chairman's parking place, stepped out of his car and did his job with no real conscience or thought as to how his Christian faith might impact it. One day, while in prayer, he had a sense that Jesus was telling him he was sick of being left in the car and wanted to come to work with him! This particular company director was a very logical, intellectual person and was somewhat taken aback by this. But the following Monday, as he got out of his car, he turned to the passenger seat and said, 'Jesus, if you want to come to work with me and make an impact on what I do here, you are very welcome.' This man had a tremendously exciting story to tell because in the following five years the way that he did business changed radically through this sense of Jesus coming to work with him. He realized that even in his Monday to Friday job, he really did have a ministry and a purpose.

Many similar stories could be told of individuals who, through their cells and their belief in every member in ministry, have come to the place of believing that God can use them. They don't have to be perfect, and they don't have to be problem free; they just need to know that they have a place and a part to play in God's body. In whatever context of life we find ourselves, whether at home with the children, at work or in church, it is the purpose of God for every believer to know that we have a ministry and can impact our environment. In other words, the nation changers of the future are not going to be just the full-time Christian leaders, but members of the whole body of Christ. There is no other way we can turn our society around. These will be the nation changers, as will be the cell leaders, who themselves will not be full-time workers but will give sacrificially of their time to shepherd and facilitate their cell members into the dreams and purposes that God has placed inside each one of them.

Out of the normal biblical beliefs that we have as Christians, and leaning on the two that we've just explored, we need to draw up some dynamic values that are at the heart of what is being called the cell movement. There are many values that we could explore, but we will look at just seven:

1. Jesus
2. every member in ministry
3. personal growth
4. multiplication
5. community
6. sacrificial love
7. honesty

1. Jesus

The first value, and probably the most obvious, is that church ought to be about Jesus. The underlying thrust of everything we do should be people meeting with Jesus and being changed by him. We want every church member to be regularly encountering the presence of the living Christ, whether through Scripture, being prayed for, seeing God through other members of the church or experiencing him personally.

Some of us may remember the Jesus Movement of the early 1970s, or may even have met some of the Jesus People around that time. There may have been a few things wrong with that movement, but one thing was very right: that an individual's faith was based on a vital encounter with Jesus. If any of us were to look at our own testimonies, or listen to stories of other people's journeys into faith, we would find that the key moments of change and growth were their encounters with God. So where are people going to encounter Jesus? If they are to encounter him in the cell church, he has to be at the heart of every cell. Jesus said, 'For where two or three come together in my name, there am I with them' (Matthew 18:20).

It is to be hoped that through everything that happens in cell life, whether it is the weekly meeting or caring for each other during the week, people will be able to encounter Jesus, and in meeting Jesus they will be changed. There could be many spring-boards that will open up these Jesus encounters. It might be in a worship time, when through a simple prayer or Scripture reading, someone is deeply moved and sees afresh the wonder of God. It might be when they are looking at Scripture together, and someone shares what a particular Bible verse or passage means to them. This could deeply impact another person, and as a result they might meet with Jesus. Or it might be during a time of ministry when someone has asked for prayer and has made themselves vulnerable. As that person is prayed for, God begins a process in their lives that impacts them and continues in the days ahead. At the same time, a person praying for someone else, giving sacrificially to them, may draw closer to Christ as a result.

Or it might be through pain. As a cell member shares a personal cause of pain with the group – maybe a marriage difficulty or problems at work – the group reaches out together with and for that person and takes that pain to God. They then, both individually and corporately, experience God's heart and love for those in pain.

2. Every member in ministry

The second value that underlines cell church is every member in ministry. In the average church, 80 per cent of the work is done by 20 per cent of the people. Deep down we must all know that if this is the case, the church will never fulfil its God-given mandate of mission and evangelism.

There is a great deal of talk about revival. This is a good thing. Manifestations of the Holy Spirit are seen as signs of this revival. However, if we look into the vitality of the early church and study church history, we will see that perhaps there is another vital ingredient, and that is the mobilization of each member of the body of Christ into their ministry. The keys to revival are surely the equipping and empowering of individual members, along with an outpouring of the Holy Spirit.

Why is it that churches have for so long talked about every member in ministry, but so poorly delivered it? Perhaps there are two reasons for this. First of all, churches may have had that as a technical belief, but not allowed it to become a dynamic value that has changed their structures. Even in structures with small groups, the groups are often led by well-meaning but slightly dominant individuals who do most of the talking and sharing, while the rest are spectators. Where churches have a strong focus on the congregational meeting, every member in ministry will be difficult to achieve.

Second, individuals often suffer from a low self-image. This is particularly true in the United Kingdom. If you were to do a survey in an average congregation and ask, 'How many of you suffer from a negative picture of yourself, feel inadequate, or reckon you have little to give?' you would be shocked at the response. If people were really honest, you would see more than 50 per cent put their hands up. Building up people's self-image is crucially important, but it will not be without difficulty. It will take a great deal of preaching, a lot of praying and much patience within the cell until people can begin to break out of the cultural, and perhaps even spiritual, bondages that have held them back from believing they have something significant to contribute. It will take time for them to go from believing that they are nothing to believing that they have something important inside them; that there are things that only they can give to the life of their church and to the life of our nation.

So much talent, so many new ministries, and so many changes in the world never happen or come to full fruition because the church does not teach that every individual member has a ministry and a purpose.

So the cell is a place where even the youngest Christian is involved, not only in the process of being discipled, but also in the process of giving out and being an active cell member. This key value pervades many of the structures and ideas of cell church. Surely we do not want to see a church of spectators, but a church of participants.

3. Personal growth

The growth of every member is our third value. Not only do we want to see individuals involved in the life of the cell, we want to create an atmosphere where there is the underlying presupposition that all members of the church should be growing, in their faith in God and in their Christian service. This value has to be outworked in a sensitive way, otherwise it could be misused. The shepherding movement of the early 1970s believed in the personal growth of every member, but it sought to impose it, through structures and onerous disciplines, onto its members. We want to create an environment that encourages spiritual growth by providing good training and equipping. We will need to use our imagination to find new ways to train people, whatever their educational background.

However, we also want to be realistic. Spiritual growth is rarely a continuous curve upwards; it looks more like a range of mountains with peaks and valleys. The truth is that many of us have been through times of real pain and difficulty, and at those times our Christian life is not about growth but more about sheer survival. So we should be realistic and sympathetic to the mountain range experiences we all go through, but within that, and over a period of time, we want a value that says, 'Just taking the easy road, just plateauing off, is not the discipleship way.' We see this enthusiasm in the life of John Wesley. In 1760 he wrote in his diary, 'I go to Bristol to purge the church of lukewarm and half-hearted members.' If that was done in any of our churches today (and I would advise that this is not a good idea) it would have bad press in the secular newspapers the following day. But it is perhaps no surprise that, with this underlying enthusiasm for spiritual growth, the early non-conformists changed our nation. Secular historians have a growing respect for what the non-conformists achieved and how they took their faith into every area of society, bringing many lasting and positive changes.

4. Multiplication

Right at its heart, a cell church has the value of multiplication. Cells, over a given period of time, should multiply. Cells should be winning people to Christ through their individual networks. Evangelism and personal mission are not optional extras: they are not activities that the church does once or twice a year; they are the life of the church.

If a cell church over a period of time isn't multiplying, if it isn't winning people to Christ, then it probably isn't a cell church yet – it is still in a state of transformation. In future chapters we will explore the whole value of multiplication in greater detail. It is crucial that we get this right, so that we can really see a dynamic change in the church – so that individual Christians are no longer cut off, but have many life-giving relationships and contacts in the world. Through these contacts, many people will slowly but surely be influenced for Christ.

5. Community

Jesus said, 'By this all men will know that you are my disciples, if you love one another' (John 13:35).

In the world today we have two main trends. One is globalization, where in many ways cultures across the world are blending together: the same youth music that is heard in London is also heard in Delhi; travel, leisure and business give us a common worldwide framework. At the same time, societies are fragmenting. People have lost their sense of belonging and identity. We are seeing, at a national level, a new sense of ethnicity. We are seeing not just one youth culture but many. Into this fragmentation is an opportunity for us to be truly prophetic. Cell church is not merely about cell meetings – it is about community. As things fragment in the big picture, people are looking for a sense of community. Within society as a whole, there are more and more small interest groups of people who have an identity, a whole load of small cultural groups, each with its own dress and its own ethos. In the midst of this confusion and fragmentation, the world is looking for people who genuinely care for one another, who will look after each other in good times and bad. Church must be about community. This cannot be done in a large gathering.

The cell provides a place where community can be built. In a cell of, say, 13 to 14 people, if someone is in financial need, they will give to one another. If they have a practical need, they will seek to fulfil it if possible. It is a place where the problems of one become the problems of them all, where the pain of one becomes the pain of them all, a place where people belong, and where love is not just a word, but a living reality. The community that we want to build in a cell should seek not only to reach out to the Christian cell members, but also be a dynamic community that includes the unchurched friends of those cell members. Through many of the activities that we will talk about in a later chapter, whether through cell members having parties or hanging out with their friends, the unchurched friends of the cell become a part of the cell community long before they attend a meeting. They begin to get a sense that their Christian friend is part of something special. Their stereotyped picture of church as a negative, institutionalized and boring place, is broken down. They also become the beneficiaries of this extended community. Maybe they have a practical need and their Christian friend can't meet it, but he or she knows someone in their cell who can. They are invited to social events that the cell puts on and are included in the fun and friendship. They begin to find that even though they don't believe in the same Christ as yet, they have a sense of belonging. They are experiencing Christian community.

The secular prophets so often point the way before we the church respond. Whether it is on green issues or how women are treated, we lag far behind. Perhaps it won't be long before the secular prophets begin to speak of the need of the community, and that the individualism of our modern society is not the healthy thing it is cracked up to be. So let us embrace the value of community and beat the secular prophets to it. Let us speak loud and clear that individuals were created by God for relationships – not for individualism, isolationism and self-sufficiency.

6. Sacrificial love

The word 'love' means many things to many people, but we want the cells to express a biblical concept of love. In our world today, we understand the love of mutuality. In other words, I will like you if you like me, or I will love you in the context of my marriage provided that this marriage works, provided that we get on well, and provided that we feel good about each other. In other contexts, friendships are formed on this same kind of tacit agreement.

However, in the New Testament, love is pictured in a totally different way. The gospel stories hinge around a cross and the sacrifice of God himself on that cross. The love of the New Testament is a love of sacrifice. You could say that this kind of love is doing what is right when you would rather do what is wrong. Love is being faithful to someone even though you would prefer to be unfaithful. Love is caring for somebody when really they're being very unpleasant and don't deserve anything. Love is speaking and living the truth when it would be much more convenient to tell a lie. Love is being patient, when that's the last thing in the world you want to be. Without having sacrificial love at the heart of church – without it as a value on which we build church and cells – we will never achieve our goal of obeying the commands of Christ. In other words, it is crucial for the transitioning of a cell church that, individually and corporately, people grasp the true value of love. No matter how hard we seek to get the right mix of people in groups, we will inevitably have people in these small communities who will not naturally like one another. They might even end up in the cell group from hell!

We are all guilty of looking at individuals from an external point of view, being put off by their character traits and cultural background, which may be different from ours. However, we must be prepared to try to see the best in people. The New Testament shows us a picture of people who lived sacrificially, not only in terms of giving practical resources, but also in terms of giving their time and energy to the work of the kingdom. Many paid the ultimate sacrifice by giving their lives.

We live in a society of consumerism, which encourages us to think only of ourselves. 'What can I get out of this?' Even the church is influenced by consumerism. We go to a church or cell meeting and evaluate it on how it blesses us, rather than on what we have contributed. Surely it is fundamental to the teachings of Christ that 'whoever wants to save his life will lose it, but whoever loses his life for me will save it' (Luke 9:24).

7. Honesty

The last value in our list is honesty. Watchman Nee, a well-known Christian from China, said that honesty is the foundation of Christianity. Cell life depends on honesty. Without honesty, it is hard to build community. Honesty opens up the doorway for people to care, and leads to personal freedom. It is interesting to note that most modern psychologists will tell us (and this is reflected in the most up-to-date treatment programmes) that honesty is the start of healing. For the Christian, honesty is the doorway to allow God into our lives, by his Spirit, through his word, and through the care of our brothers and sisters in Christ.

So often we are afraid of being honest. Our world tells us that if we are honest, people will despise us and look down on us. At the time of the sad death of Diana, Princess of Wales, a number of commentators were trying to explain the huge public response to this extraordinary lady. They said that it had a great deal to do with her honesty. It is extremely unusual in our modern society for an important figure to publicly confess to personal struggles, failings and weaknesses, as she did. But rather than being rejected, her honesty and frankness won people's hearts. Surely this is an important lesson.

Honesty does not cause people to reject us. In fact, the very reverse is true. It helps people to understand who we are and where we come from, and it helps them reach out to us. If we are really going to grasp this value of honesty, we must help our church members resist the pressure of society, which all the time is encouraging us, in big ways and small, to be dishonest and hide who we really are. Many of our church members are carrying around great burdens of pain, internal struggles and areas of darkness in their lives. If, through honesty with God and the help of caring cell members, they could be pulled into the light, they would be set free.

'But if we walk in the light, as he is in the light, we have fellowship with one another, and the blood of Jesus, his Son, purifies us from all sin' (1 John 1:7). This scripture unpacks the double impact of honesty. Not only does honesty give us fellowship with one another and help to build community, it is also a doorway to cleansing, to spiritual forgiveness and spiritual power.

For example, in one cell meeting, Henry began to share how he had always felt pressurized to be successful. He had spent most of his life seeking success and he always compared himself with others. As Henry shared this and as he was prayed for, a process of freedom began in his life. He realized that God was calling him to be faithful, and not to compare himself with others. A little bit of honesty had set him free from years of striving into a sense of peace and a new purpose.

Without our church grasping the value of honesty, it will be very hard work for ourselves. Honesty creates the environment for love and acceptance, and for the power of God to break in and touch us.

In closing this segment on values, there is a secret value of cell church that we would want to mention: intentionality. In other words, having decided that we believe certain things and that these values are radically important to us, we now have to, on a continuing basis, month after month, year after year, keep these beliefs and values and systems working in the life of our church. Change does not just happen. We have to co-operate and work with the Holy Spirit on an ongoing basis to put these things into practice, recognizing all the time that it is the nature of church life that things unwind. One of the most important things we have to do as leaders is to be continually intentional about what we feel God is leading us into.

Summary

- Cell is church. The cell has the double mandate of discipleship and evangelism. As many of the functions of church as possible are carried out in the life of the community making up the cell group.
- A cell church has both cell and celebration, with cell as the primary building block.
- Every member of the body of Christ has a contribution to make, using their gifts to minister both in the church and out of it.
- The values of cell church are:
  1. Jesus

2. every member in ministry
3. personal growth
4. multiplication
5. community
6. sacrificial love
7. honesty

3

Evangelism Values

A key distinction of a cell church is that it works on a different understanding of evangelism from the one that so often springs to mind. In very simple terms, cell-based evangelism is network evangelism. It is every member of that cell having a number of local, unchurched friends whom they are getting to know. These relationships need to progress to a level whereby the unbelievers can see a demonstration of radical Christian life and where confidence is built to allow the Christians to share about Jesus. The role of the cell is to empower that cell member into these relationships, and to hold them accountable to them. In other words, we are enabling each other to obey the commands of Christ, and one of these commands is to love the lost. Over a period of time, the cell, both corporately and individually, will encourage each person to make friends with the unchurched and to reach out to them with action, love and words.

If we are going to redefine evangelism, giving greater emphasis to network and creative evangelism and truly motivating each person to do this, we need a new understanding. We need

NETWORK EVANGELISM

To understand network evangelism we must understand the shift that has taken place and the new paradigm relating to evangelism.

OLD PARADIGM	NEW PARADIGM
Truth	Relational truth
Decision	Process
Winning	Keeping
Few	Many
Evangelist	Cell

The parable of the sower in Matthew 13 outlines the nature of process evangelism and how understanding and honesty are the key issues in the evangelistic process. Some 70 per cent of people come to faith through relationships.

THE GHETTOIZATION OF THE CHURCH

How do we get out of it? The end goal is for each Christian to have unchurched relationships. The cell empowers and holds each member accountable to these relationships and supports them through activities. The bigger church also empowers, holds reaping meetings and organizes 'Alpha' in service to the cells and their individual members.

to jettison the unhelpful pictures that people might have of evangelism, which actually make it difficult for them to participate.

In recent years there has been a paradigm shift in the Christian understanding of our culture and how we can reach out appropriately.

Paradigm

A paradigm is a set of principles and ideas we have inside us that affects our outward actions. For example, in the twelfth and thirteenth centuries, there was a general belief that the world was flat. Therefore, people lived with a flat world paradigm. This paradigm was not just an idea – it affected people's behaviour, particularly if they owned a boat. If you had a boat and lived in a flat world paradigm, you did not sail too far because you might fall off the edge of the world. But a revolution was growing – it was the 'world is round' paradigm, which was finally proved by Christopher Columbus. With the acceptance of the new paradigm, there was a change of action: a new age of exploration began and the world has never been the same.

Here is another example. At the end of the nineteenth century, a group of scientists discovered germs, therefore creating the germ paradigm. Doctors and surgeons have, from that day on, paid tribute to the existence of the germ paradigm by washing their hands before surgery. This paradigm has impacted medical practices ever since.

In the same way, there is a changing paradigm in the area of evangelism. Let us look at an old and a new paradigm – bearing in mind that we are not knocking the old paradigm of evangelism, because in its day it worked. But the world has dramatically changed since then, and we need to change our approach with it.

In the old paradigm, evangelism was about telling people the truth. Evangelists found as many opportunities as they could, in as many creative ways as possible, to tell people the truth. Churches had special meetings, called gospel services, in which they proclaimed the truth. Brave Christians told their friends the truth. A parody of this is to say, 'I have the truth and you don't, but you are about to receive it.' In its day, and in the right context, it worked. In some nations, it might still work today. But in the Western world, we have seen a radical change: the arrival of postmodernity. Today, most people under the age of 35 don't believe there is such a thing as objective, consistent truth; they believe that truth is relative, and all truths are equally valid. They find their truth through personal experiences.

Postmodernity

What is postmodernity? In simple terms, it is a rejection of the idea that there is any absolute or objective truth, and an acceptance that the only real truth is what I personally believe and have experienced. This creates an environment where everything is right, nothing is wrong, and the only things that are really wrong are to say that 'I'm the one who's right', or to do nasty things to little children. Sociologists put it this way: the person of today does not believe in what is called the 'meta-narrative'. That is, they don't believe there is a big story that holds life together, guiding how you should behave and what you should believe. This meta-narrative could be modernism, Christianity, communism, or whatever. Today's postmodern person believes that there isn't a consistent philosophy to life, and as a result chooses a pick-and-mix philosophy. Since they believe there is no big story, it doesn't matter if the component parts of their belief system are in conflict and inconsistent with each other. This is a radical change from anything we have seen in the past. Perhaps I can explain. The behaviour of a classic 1960s rebel may be very similar to the behaviour of a young person today. But the difference is this: the 1960s rebel was by definition moving away from something that he or she understood; they were making a conscious choice to behave differently from what was expected, according to the influence of the meta-narrative of their background. The young person of today is just behaving; they have made no conscious, rational choice to walk away from anything.

The postmodern environment creates several opportunities for evangelism, but also many problems. For example, spirituality is now back on the agenda: whereas the modernist had a worldview that was basically atheistic and man-centred, the postmodern person is open to all sorts of ideas, including spirituality. Hence we see the rise of things like New Age spirituality. In one sense, this makes evangelism easier, as people do not rule out the existence of faith and God automatically. However, discipleship will be a lot harder.

Discipleship

Discipleship is the spiritual journey that Jesus encouraged us all to be on, so that we might be conformed into his image and be changed. Jesus commanded his disciples to make not converts but disciples – people who will walk with God and grow in their Christian life. In today's world, discipleship is a lot more difficult because the postmodern environment encourages what we might call enthusiastic dualism. This is where we behave in a certain way in one environment, but in a totally different way in another environment. It has always been a challenge in the church to encourage Christians to be consistent in every area of their lives. However, today it has become more difficult because generally there is no acceptance of truth. Therefore, people's consciences are a lot more hardened, and an individual's inconsistent behaviour does not bring the sense of conviction and wrongdoing that it might previously have done.

Twenty years ago, you could have had a Christian young person sleeping with their boyfriend or girlfriend, and being rebellious in that sense – in other words, dualistic. But they would almost certainly have been non-enthusiastic in the Christian part of their lives. You would have seen their dualism in the way they did not worship and in their general demeanour and attitude. But today's postmodern dualist Christian teenager can be really enthusiastic about Jesus, be the keenest member of the youth group and take part wholeheartedly in Christian activities. Unfortunately, in the other part of their lives, they can participate with equal enthusiasm in drug-taking, sleeping around and rebellious behaviour of all sorts. This is because they have compartmentalized their lives, and it doesn't matter to them if there is inconsistency with their pick-and-mix philosophy. As you can see, this sort of attitude makes discipleship a great deal harder.

If cells had no other reason for their existence, this would be good enough. Surely there is no other way to get people to confront their enthusiastic dualism and hold one another accountable than in a loving atmosphere where they encounter truth and understanding.

Relational truth

If telling people the truth does not have the power it used to because of postmodernity, how are we going to reach them? The new paradigm is about relational truth. It is still a truth that sets people free. The gospel message is a big story – it is all about truth. But how do we communicate it to the world of today? The answer is, it has to be relationally carried so that it can be experienced, touched and seen before people believe. In other words, we Christians who carry the truth must have that truth as a reality in our own lives. We will then be in contact with our unchurched world, and our friends, colleagues and acquaintances will have an opportunity to touch and see the truth in us. People will hear the truth in the right and appropriate manner, and in this way they can be radically converted.

In a sense, we could argue that this is the difference between the Old and New Testaments. If we were to ask ourselves what the epoch moment of truth is in the Old Testament, we would probably say that it is God's covenant and the giving of the Law. It was an objective revelation that came from God and said to us 'this is right' and 'that is wrong'. In the New Testament, we see God taking a whole new approach to truth: 'The Word became flesh and made his dwelling among us. We have seen his glory, the glory of the One and Only, who came from the Father, full of grace and truth' (John 1:14). So truth had invaded the world and could be touched, seen and felt in the person of Jesus. It was incarnational truth. Jesus took a radical approach. He did not just tell people the truth – he said that if they wanted to know the truth, they should follow him, as he is the truth. The truth still had a certain objectivity to it, but in another sense it had to be experienced by following Jesus. At the end of his life, Jesus commissioned his disciples to go out, living and speaking the truth, because the truth would be in them by the power of the Holy Spirit.

In the ghetto

Hopefully, we can see that if we are going to impact our society, we must get out of our Christian ghettos.

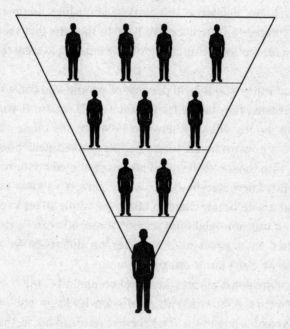

In looking at the above diagram, we see that so often we start our Christian lives with many unchurched friends, but the longer we believe, the fewer we have. Soon we reach that moment of ultimate 'sanctification' where we have no non-Christian friends.

It might be important to note – especially as there is a lot of talk about revival – that in many places where revival broke out there were two very interesting characteristics. First, there were relational communities. Second, people worked where they lived. One of the things people might say when they read this is, 'But I have lots of unchurched friends.' The trouble is, so often these people are friends in our work environment, and many of us don't work where we live. Even if we did, our friends might not live where they work. In our modern culture, we might travel to work. But there is little evidence to say that people will travel to church. So, in a sense, our work relationships become a missionary aspect of our lives. We have to face the fact that if we want to see our local churches grow, we must build local relationships.

John Finney said that 70 per cent of people who come to faith do so because they have a friend who is a Christian. If you go to a Welsh mining village where the 1904 revivals broke out, you will see an environment where people worked near home and where, with those little terraced houses crammed up the hillsides, everybody knew everybody. So when a person who was a drunkard and a wife beater came to faith, the whole street knew. But today, in our non-relational society, somebody can be radically converted in a street and it makes no difference to anyone because we don't know our neighbours.

There are some places where real community still exists. But they are rare. A Youth With A Mission leader in one of these places took his dog to the vet. When he returned home, there was a knock at the door. A little old lady asked him how his dog was. He responded by informing her that the dog was well. Then he asked her, 'How do you know about my dog?'

She replied, 'Young man, if I don't know it, it hasn't happened.' Unfortunately this is not the community of today for most of us. If it were, our evangelism would be a great deal more effective.

However, there is one group of people who have the hallmarks of this kind of revival sociology – a group who live where they work and who know everybody. These are our teenagers. There will be more about this group later. Another place to have seen revival in modern times is the Hebridean islands. Here too is a highly relational community where people live and work in the same place.

There are two implications for us. First, we must get out of our Christian ghettos and into relationships with local people. Second, we need to believe that the gospel, the truth, will impact people through our relationships.

Decisions versus process

We have seen that the old paradigm of evangelism was about telling people the truth, but the new paradigm is about relational truth. In the same way, the old paradigm of evangelism was about getting people to make a decision. All our effort was aimed towards getting decisions for Christ. Evangelism was about how many had made the decision – this was the success or failure factor.

In the new paradigm, evangelism is not about a decision; it is a process. Of course, within this process there is a decision. But we have to understand that if we live in a postmodern society, most people will have a negative picture of God and the church. Before they can be asked to believe in Jesus, they need to have their underlying concepts changed as to who God is and what the church is like. In understanding that evangelism is a process, we begin to realize that there is a lot of work that can and must be done before people can make an effective decision.

'Even now the reaper draws his wages, even now he harvests the crop for eternal life, so that the sower and the reaper may be glad together. Thus the saying "One sows and another reaps" is true' (John 4:36–37). Here Jesus talks about sowing and reaping.

In the context of the passage, the Samaritan woman had just had a new experience of God. It was Jesus who had completed the sowing and reaping process, and through him she had taken a step into the kingdom. But who had done the sowing? It was her Samaritan culture; it was the prophets of old. This lady already believed in one God, in a coming Messiah, and in worship. Her life may not have been consistent with these beliefs, but she did have within her a fairly positive picture of God. In a sense, all she needed was some proof that this underlying belief was true. Jesus convinced her of this and she believed.

In our modern society, before we reap, we must sow. If we imagine a scale of 1 to 10, where 1 is very negative and 10 is conversion based on a positive picture of God and the church, suddenly evangelism radically changes. Evangelism is not just the step from 9 to 10, the decision. If, through our relationships with people, they go from 1 to 2 and their view of God becomes more positive, that's evangelism as well.

Keeping people

Another drawback of the old paradigm of winning people was that once they had made the decision, our evangelistic interest drained away. For example, in Europe when the wall between East and West came down, many evangelists went into eastern Europe, held big meetings, saw literally hundreds of thousands of people come to Christ, then left. Unfortunately, many of these evangelists did not leave literature in the language of the people and did not work through indigenous churches. Al Akimoff, a long-time church worker in eastern Europe and the USSR, called these evangelists the 'Christian plunderers'. Fortunately not everybody did this. But many did.

In the new paradigm, the emphasis is on keeping people. Obviously a decision is important, but that is just the beginning. Jesus wants us not to go out and make converts, but to make disciples. If we have this 'keep' mentality in our minds, then right from the beginning of our evangelistic enterprises we will be asking ourselves, 'When these people come to Christ, who will look after them, how will they be looked after, and how can we build God's church here?' Our goal is to see each convert become a part of the body of Christ and find their identity in that body as an active member.

In the old paradigm, evangelism was done by the heroic few who stood on street corners, knocked on doors and stirred up everyone to find ways to share their faith. To have been one of the few was probably a wonderful thing. However, in the new paradigm, evangelism is about the many; it is about every single Christian believing they can be a part of the sowing and reaping process. It is only the mobilization of the many that can cause the church to really grow.

As long as people see evangelism as a decision, we will not see people being mobilized to do the work. But if Christians recognize that evangelism is a process, then everybody will feel they can take part – that they can make friends with non-Christians and take the opportunities God presents to them. In that sense, it doesn't really matter if a person gives their life to the Lord in a meeting, on their own, or in a one-to-one way with their friend – as long as they do it.

Surely the mobilizing of the church in terms of every member being involved is the most crucial issue facing us at this time. In the old paradigm, when the gospel was preached and we listened to the content, in many cases the content majored on the benefits of the gospel. In other words, how we could be forgiven, how we could have new life with God, a clean sheet, an eternal hope, and so on. In a culture that understands the full implications of Christianity, this type of preaching may be very effective. But in the new paradigm, we want to look at the content of the gospel as it relates to a more postmodern culture.

Postmodernity encourages people in self-determination; they are in control of their lives; they choose what is right and wrong; they decide for themselves what they do and do not believe. In this context, it is easy to hear a gospel message that concentrates on forgiveness and new life and to accept it. They try to live in the benefits of Christianity while ultimately remaining in control of their lives. As you can see, this is not the whole of the gospel message, just part of it.

In the new paradigm we have to preach a gospel that is focused on 2 Corinthians 5:15: '. . . he died for all, that those who live should no longer live for themselves but for him who died for them and was raised again.' The real issue is: 'Who is in control?' Surely becoming a Christian involves giving our lives back to God and surrendering our self-control, our ability to choose for ourselves what is right and wrong, and placing Christ and his truth at the centre. We are not doing our own thing, but his thing. We have given away the ownership of our lives. This is the message we need in our self-centred world today. Out of this, people can experience wonderful forgiveness and cleansing.

Jesus

Finally, in the old paradigm there was the correct assumption that people knew a great deal about God and Christ. When we talked about the gospel, we often spoke about the means by which people could come to faith, about the cross and about repentance. In the new paradigm, we need to talk a lot more about Jesus.

Paul said, 'For I resolved to know nothing while I was with you except Jesus Christ and him crucified' (1 Corinthians 2:2). In our society, where structured Christianity is a bit of a turn-off, maybe we need to do a lot more talking and preaching about the most wonderful person who ever lived: Jesus the Son of God. We need to tell the Jesus stories. We should enthral people with his goodness, kindness and sacrifice. If we lift him up, will not people be drawn to him?

The old paradigm was empowered by the evangelist. The evangelists were the heroes. But the new paradigm is empowered by the cell. It is the cell, meeting on a regular basis, that seeks to bring each cell member out of their Christian ghetto and into relationships with the unchurched. So the cell becomes the pivotal point in empowerment and accountability in the area of evangelism. As for the biblical basis for this, apart from the reasons already mentioned (i.e. the New Testament model of incarnational truth and Jesus' command to his disciples to make disciples), we could look in Matthew 13 at the parable of the sower. This parable – which is also found in Mark and Luke – is agreed by many theologians to be not only one of the primary parables in the New Testament, but also a very significant parable when it comes to understanding evangelism. In this parable, we see two distinct concepts – good soil and bad soil, or good converts and bad converts – and the parable helps us understand the difference between the two. At the end of the parable, we see the 'good soil' convert, the person who has come to faith and produced good fruit in their lives. This is the type of convert we are looking for. But we also see in the parable the 'rocky soil' convert: someone who receives the message with great joy, gets really excited about following Jesus, but after a short period of time falls away. We also see another 'bad soil' convert who seems to last longer, but eventually the weeds and the thorns choke them and they fall away as well. So what is this all about? Jesus tells us that the bad soil represents people who don't understand. In other words, the path, the rocky soil, and the thorny soil symbolize different levels of not understanding.

There are people out there who understand nothing about the gospel. They have a very negative picture of Jesus and the church, and they are not liable to respond at this time. However, the rocky soil obviously represents someone who does understand something of the Christian message – most likely the benefits – but they don't understand it is going to cost them something. The 'thorny soil' convert does not understand that being a Christian is not just about having a part of their lives touched by the Spirit of God, but includes everything, particularly their attitude to money and how they relate to the world. The gospel message is a holistic message for the whole of life and is in direct contrast to the pick-and-mix philosophy of today.

We could ask whose fault it is that we so often see 'rocky soil' converts, people who believe for a moment but then fall away. Surely we, the church, must take responsibility for this, because we have not made sure that people really understand what it means to be a Christian before they make the decision. This is particularly important in our postmodern world. A good biblical example of this is the difference in approaches between the apostle Peter in Jerusalem and Paul in Athens. When Peter preached in Jerusalem, people cried out, 'How can we be saved?' and thousands were added to the church. Peter was speaking to people who largely understood a one God, Judaic mindset. They had heard and seen Jesus when he was alive. This meant that Peter could preach for a decision. When the apostle Paul preached in Athens, however, he saw a different response. Once the people had heard him, they said, 'Can we come and talk to you more about this?' They had a lot further to go on their journey. They came from a pagan mindset, with many gods and many influences, and they needed to understand what it meant to be a Christian.

In looking at the 'good soil' convert, we see that there are two crucial ingredients to conversion: honesty and understanding. If you understand, but are not prepared to be honest and admit you've gone against God's ways, you won't be converted. Isn't that what this parable is trying to say? Your hearers might think that they want to change, and they might give their lives to Christ, but without understanding the full implications. They are not being honest with themselves, and this parable indicates that they may well fall away. So, out of this parable we get a theological basis for evangelism as a process. People need to be honest about themselves and then, out of their understanding and honesty, give their hearts to Christ.

Alpha

Question: What new paradigm method of evangelism has impacted the church in a big way in the last few years? Answer: Alpha. Most of the ingredients of the new paradigm can be found in Alpha: it is relational; it is about people understanding what the Christian faith is about before making a decision; it is about the many being involved, then bringing their friends to the next Alpha course.

So are evangelists redundant in the cell system and the new

paradigm? I don't think so. Whether through Alpha, or whether through events that are put on at our church, there are still particularly gifted individuals who are good at the reaping part of evangelism – helping people to come to that honest moment and give their lives to Christ. Unfortunately, though, the church has sometimes relied on these far more than it should have done. Cell church evangelism, as we have said already, should involve every member making friends with the unchurched, being in a process with them, being empowered by the cell during that process, and doing it out of a genuine compassion and love for their friends, not just to see someone converted. At the right time, they will bring their friends into contact with Jesus – be it through an Alpha course, through their own conversations, through special meetings, or through taking them to hear an evangelist whereby people have the opportunity to give their lives to Christ.

Summary

- Cell-based evangelism is network evangelism.
- The role of the cell is to empower cell members into building relationships with unchurched people who live locally. The cell holds the members accountable to reach out through relationship.
- Evangelism in a postmodern culture is no longer a truth encounter, as there is a rejection of any absolute truth. Instead a pick-and-mix culture allows for enthusiastic dualism.
- The message needs to focus on who is in control, and the person of Jesus.
- The gospel has to be relationally carried, so that it can be experienced before it is believed. The challenge for Christians is to live out the truth in a manner that is transparent to an unbe-

liever – to be an incarnation of the truth and to believe that the gospel will impact people through relationship.

- In order to see the unchurched become Christians, Christians must get out of the Christian ghetto and make relationships within the communities where they live.

- In the new paradigm, evangelism is not a decision but has become a process whereby the unchurched are gradually moved away from having a negative picture of God and the church.

- It is not enough to win people; they need to be nurtured and added to the church.

4

The Transitioning Process and the Prototype Cell

Transition means change – getting from here to there. So if the idea of cell church has caught your imagination, if its theology and values are something you believe in, how do you take your church from where it is now towards becoming a cell church?

Danger

First, I should let you know that there are dangers along the way. Whatever you do, avoid the ICC syndrome: Instant Cell Church.

There are some quite simple structures in the idea of cell church, so it is easy to fall into the temptation of implementing these structures without the necessary preparation. This will inevitably form legalism, and it is not the way to go. Also, the cell movement itself should never become a bandwagon, with everybody leaping on; the easier it is for people to leap on, the easier it will be for them to leap off.

What is transition about?

In thinking about transition, you might want to look at a process like this:

Beliefs → Vision → Values → Transition → Cell church.

It is important to understand this process in any type of change – whether you are asking an individual to repent, change their life and come into discipleship, or you are asking a group of people to change the structures that might be very precious to them. One of the striking things in the New Testament is the word 'repentance'. This is the key change word. Often, in our modern interpretation of this word, we see it as a leap to action but, as many theologians will tell us, the original word in the Greek texts (*metanoeo*) means 'to change your mind'. It could also mean 'to change your value systems'. So often individuals are encouraged to change their behaviour, but in their heads they still have the world's value systems. Understandably, they end up quite confused.

Perhaps we could use a computer analogy. It is like having an operating system called World 95, and you try to run Kingdom of God programs within that operating system. The programs may function, but not at their best. We need a new operating system, called Kingdom of God 2000, and within this we can run Kingdom of God programs properly. They will work so much better.

Changing people's values is often the missing key in effective discipleship. We so often create an environment that conforms and changes people's behaviour, but once people are out of that environment – be it a lively youth group, or a dynamic church – they can revert all too easily. However, if we encourage people to embrace God's value systems in all parts of their life, their values will shape their actions.

This is exactly true when it comes to transition into a cell church. The change starts with 'What do you believe?', not only with doctrine, but also in terms of belief about church. Out of our beliefs comes a new set of values: Jesus at the centre; every member in ministry; every member growing; multiplication through relational evangelism; sacrificial love; community, and honesty. Then out of these beliefs and values will come a new vision of church. This is cell church vision: a small group of people who see that they are church. They have a responsibility to pastor one another, and to empower one another for Christian living and evangelism. These dynamic cells may meet together in celebration in large groups, to be taught and inspired further. This is not church as we've known it, with its bias towards Sundays and congregational structures, towards only about 20 per cent of the people doing the work, towards wanting to do evangelism but not knowing how, and towards wanting to empower people in the market-place, but again not knowing how it could happen.

In our church there may be structures – for example, a coun-selling system, or a homeless project – that we might want to keep, and these can be incorporated into the cell vision. There may be other structures, on the other hand, that compete with the cell – mid-week Bible studies, or prayer meetings that might need to go. We want to keep our vision of a church that is mobi-lized and encountering Jesus on an individual basis. This vision has within it the ingredients that could lead to revival; it could result in an intensity of the Holy Spirit creating life-changing encounters with God. More than that, revival is not just an inten-sity of the Holy Spirit, it is a mobilization of the whole body of Christ. The great need of the church today is to mobilize – it is necessary for every member to say, 'I have a part to play. I can make a difference.' A mobilized church is a church which knows that, to complete the task, it needs more of God; it is a dependent church, which calls down and receives more of the intensity of the Holy Spirit. In turn, that intensity leads to more mobilization. Maybe this is what revival really looks like.

So, within the transition process, a few leaders and key church people need to have a dynamic vision that comes from their beliefs and values being refocused and changed. But then comes a 'danger moment'! These enthused leaders, who want to see results and change, and probably want to see them today, could leap straight into the new structure and impose it upon the church at large. The fresh ideas, the new vision and all the structures that relate to it will be pushed onto the people, without them experiencing the process of change that the leaders have gone through. So transition is about the church at large having an opportunity to readjust its beliefs and values, to fully embrace those beliefs and values, and to have an excitement about the vision. This will then give people the willingness to let go of the ideas, structures and traditions that may have been with them for many, many years. It is important for leaders to treat the congregations with respect, and lead with gentleness and patience.

Changing

In practical terms, how do we begin to change the larger group? Having read this book and other books on cell church, leaders can start to speak out through their preaching opportunities, communicating their new beliefs about church. They can take the opportunity in the months ahead to preach, teach and publicly explore the seven values that uphold cell church:

Teaching and Preaching Relating to the Values

1. Jesus at the centre

Characterized by the life of the disciple, obedience to Jesus and development of faith, which involves having confidence in God and an expectation that he will work.

Topics:
- Personal prayer.
- Corporate prayer.
- Receiving our worth from Christ.
- Jesus as the centre reference point of our daily lives.
- The Bible as the foundation of the plumb-line.
- Biblical teaching requires a response from those who hear it.
- Reflecting the character of Jesus with emphasis on being unselfish, loving unconditionally, giving and receiving forgiveness.

2. Every member in ministry

Characterized by encouraging every member to know their gifts and be prepared to use them in the context of the market-place, the body of Christ and in evangelism.

Topics:
- Dealing with a negative self-image.
- Stewardship of my gifts.
- Developing my gifts.

- Identifying my gifts.
- Listening to the Holy Spirit and the gifts of the Spirit.
- Understanding the salt and light mandate and my role in the market-place.

3. Every member growing

Characterized by discipleship that encourages a desire to grow and change to become like Jesus, free and whole to serve the Lord.

Topics:
- The essence of discipleship is learning more.
- The importance of the body of Christ and the cell in the process.
- Accountability and self-revelation.
- Having a Christian value system.
- Living beyond our feelings.
- Trusting God in difficult circumstances.
- Dealing with pain and disillusionment.
- A pressing-on attitude.
- Knowing God for his own worth.

4. Multiplication or relational evangelism

Characterized by recognizing God's heart for the lost and my responsibility in that.

Topics:
- Understanding relational evangelism.
- Building networks.

- Praying for my friends and the area.
- How a cell develops into community with the unchurched as a part of that.
- How to share what I believe and my experiences with God.
- How my cell will grow and multiply as new believers join the group.

5. Community

Characterized by building communities of quality relationships, of acceptance, listening, giving and receiving, trust and honesty, vulnerability and equality, which facilitate discipleship and outreach.

Topics:
- Community is something we enter into by laying down our lives.
- Real community is a place that is inclusive of believers and seekers of whatever age.
- How the cell meeting facilitates community.
- The importance of cell community having vision and goals that include making relationships with the unchurched and how we can meet their needs and see them become Christians.
- Generosity.
- Hospitality.

6. Sacrificial love

Characterized by understanding that real love is doing what is right when you'd like to do what is wrong.

Topics:
- The cross as an example of a new way to love.
- Love as a commitment.
- The role of feelings.
- How we see others.
- How God sees others.
- Practical love as demonstrated by listening and asking questions skills.
- Learning to live beyond our cultural and personal preferences.

7. Honesty

Characterized by the capacity to be real and to ask for help, and an attitude of vulnerability.

Topics:
- How to trust.
- Dealing with the fear of rejection.
- Self-worth is in Christ.
- Understanding the power of God in the body of Christ.
- How I can pray, and encourage others.
- Confidentiality.

1. What does it really mean to have Jesus at the centre of our lives and experience? How can we really encounter him? There are obviously many hours of preaching here, but some of the key elements of Jesus being at the centre of our community should be focused on.
2. Every member in ministry – what does this actually mean? Leaders should speak from Scripture and experience on how

each member can play a part. Each one of us has a role in church, in the market-place, in ministry towards one another, in evangelism and mission.

3. Every member growing – do we really believe that as Christians we should always be growing? Is there a hunger within our church for people not to live in the status quo, but to dare to believe that there is more? As we explore this value, we must be real. It is very important for leaders to remember that church members at times live in pain and disillusionment from visions that church leaders have held out to them in the past, and their personal growth can be affected by their response to church as a whole. Therefore, leaders must approach this whole process with great care. We may be deeply enthused, totally convinced this is God, but we must also be realistic. This process is going to take time. It is not going to be easy, so we must give time for people to buy into the process, to adapt to the vision and values, and we need to make sure that even though we preach the values and beliefs, we do not promise heaven on earth. We are making these changes because we believe in the ideals and principles behind cell church. We do hope that it will give a greater dynamic in the life of church. Nevertheless, perhaps we can help people see that there is a hope and that the changes will help us to obey the commands of Christ in a more dynamic and effective way.

4. Multiplication, or relational evangelism – a lot of change is needed when it comes to understanding what evangelism is and isn't. My book *Sowing and Reaping* covers this subject in further detail.

5. Community – as we work towards the cell idea, this value is very important. It is easy to allow the cell just to become a

meeting, and not to realize that we are trying to create a community. This little group of Christians must first look after one another, and then what happens in the meetings will spill out into their week in terms of caring for one another and praying for one another. What happens in the week also spills into their meeting. We want not only to create a community of Christians, but it is our vision to create a comnunity of Christians who are reaching out to their friends. So now we are creating a community that includes non-Christians who come to the parties of the cell members and to cell events, so that they are relationally a part, but do not attend cell meetings. Also, it is important, as we teach on community, that this is not something that we do; it is in fact something that we enter into. We join in a community of sacrificing members. We have an attitude of giving our lives away through hospitality and generosity, and both of these are important sub-values that can be taught on, as they are part of the building blocks of community. Then out of this hospitality and generosity come the many activities of community, sharing, caring and praying.

6. Sacrificial love – this is a crucial value. Cells will definitely not work on the basis of love by mutuality. Before the idea of cells is introduced and people are placed into cells (more on this later), leaders should make it clear that although being in a cell will benefit them, that is not why they are entering one. They will not necessarily be with their best friends. They may, in reality, be placed with one or two people they do not get on with. The cell should be a place where members learn to obey the commands of Christ and love one another. As Jesus pointed out, it is in giving that we receive: 'Whoever finds his life will lose it, and whoever loses his life for my sake will find it' (Matthew 10:39).

7. Of course, that very important value, accountability, can only really happen as people learn to be honest. Are we prepared to be honest? Can we, as leaders, in the power of God's love and Spirit, and through the teaching of God's word, break out of our reserve, face the fear of rejection (which will actually never or very rarely happen), and begin to let people know who we really are and what we are really like?

Strategies

Having seen, then, that there needs to be a process, and that the process begins with values and vision, it might be helpful for the key leaders involved to sit down and plan a strategy on how to bring about change. There are two pathways that churches can follow. The first is to set up a series of prototype cells, beginning very small and slowly but surely. The cells would then multiply out into the existing church and evangelistically into the community. The second 'big bang' transitional pathway is to train a group of potential cell leaders, and, over a relatively short period of time, put everybody in your existing church into cells.

I will consider both pathways, but concentrate on the first one as in my view it tends to be the most effective.

The first pathway: prototype cells for church leaders

The prototype strategy is recommended by Ralph Neighbour and Bill Beckham in their books on the subject. It has been the experience of a number of churches in the United Kingdom that they started with a leadership cell, where the main leaders of the church, along with their spouses, formed a cell. The cell met for about three months, and they sought to put into practice as many of the principles of cell life as possible. What happened was that the main leaders of the church experienced for themselves the power of cells and their value systems were changed. That way, as they began to speak about cells to their church, they were not just speaking out of hypothetical knowledge but from real experience.

Here in detail are the things we would want those leaders to experience.

Understanding the four 'W's

Most cells in cell churches have within them an internal structure. This internal structure is there to serve the leaders. It is there to make sure the vision and the values actually happen. In the future there will hopefully be relatively young Christians leading cells. Even though they may not have the maturity and experience that we have, they will be greatly helped by the fact that there is a loose framework to operate in.

The beauty of this framework is that it really does help us to experience the vision and values of the cell. We will also be able to train people more effectively as we will know approximately what is going to happen with the cell group. By contrast, in some previous house groups there was no clear vision or set of values that everybody was aiming at, and often every group was shaped in the image of its leader.

The four components of a cell meeting are: the welcome, the worship, the word and the witness. As we look at these within the prototype cell, we are in a sense creating a false environment, but because the people involved are leaders, or potential leaders, this is fine. It is very important that we don't just lead out of head knowledge, and that we never ask our church members to go where we have not gone ourselves. Therefore, in this prototype cell, we want to experience some of the things that the church members have to experience, so that our leadership has reality.

1. The welcome. The first 'w' is the welcome. One of the key values within cell thinking is every member in ministry. Another key value is honesty. When the cell meets, the first thing we want to do is ask everybody an open question, which in our prototype cells should be fairly demanding. We might ask a question like, 'Where did you hide as a child when life was difficult?' and through this we might learn something new about each other. Then we might ask a second question like, 'Where do you hide as an adult?' Or we could ask, 'What was your coldest physical experience?' A follow-up question might be, 'What was your coldest emotional experience?'

So what does this achieve? First, when everybody speaks, something important takes place. Everybody in that cell goes from being a spectator to a participator. Second, community has begun to form. One of the key ingredients that binds any group of people together is that they have experiences that are common to them – that they know things about one another that no one else really knows.

I was with a group of leaders once and I suggested that we do this, but my suggestion was met with great disdain. 'Oh, we've known each other for years,' they cried.

Despite this, we worked our way through a couple of questions. I asked them, 'What music most influenced you as a teenager?' And second, 'What person most influenced you, for good or bad?' In answering these, the leaders learned things about each another that amazed them, even though they had been friends for a long time.

Third, honesty begins to develop, and this is particularly true when we set up real cells and the questions are perhaps a little easier at the start. We have to engage in a process where people learn to trust each other with the mundane and the simple. This is because people will probably not share the deep needs of their lives until they can trust each other with something that is of relatively little importance. Confidentiality is crucial to a developing cell. Cell members will never learn to be open with the big and little things of life unless the cell members have agreed to this principle. We as leaders often preach about openness and honesty, but the fact is that we can be some of the most hidden people within our churches. So, both for our main church leaders and our potential cell leaders, this level of honesty is an extremely important part of our prototype experience. If we look in the book of Acts, we see that the writer, Luke, has been very honest in showing the tensions between Paul and Barnabas, and between Peter and Paul, and we see something of the tensions of the early church. So the honesty of the book of Acts needs to be a part of our everyday culture.

In the cell outlines at the end of this book, there are some suggested questions that you can use.

2. The worship.   The second 'w' is the worship. Meeting with Jesus, experiencing him and having him at the centre of our churches and our lives, is the major ingredient of the cell vision. When it comes to worship within cells, we want to suggest some perhaps new and creative ways of doing this.

For many groups of this size, worship that is musical can be quite difficult and also extremely embarrassing. Many small groups don't have musicians or people who can really sing. So we want to encourage a mix where perhaps there will be some meetings where we can worship with singing as normal, but also have

meetings where we can explore non-musical worship. One
example of this is to ask people to read John 3:16, then have a
moment of quiet so that they can think about one thing that
strikes them from this verse. Then, ask people to share their
thoughts and insights. Conclude with a time of open prayer,
where people give thanks for what they have learned through this
about the nature and wonder of God.

Again, in the cell outlines at the end of this book, we have
included some suggested non-musical worship ideas. Also we
would recommend *50 Worship Ideas for Small Groups* by Stuart
Townend.

This kind of worship actually demands more participation
from the members, as well as more creativity. Then, when we
worship in the big group on a Sunday, we will have the joy of
worshipping God through a medium we have perhaps not used
in the cell: singing and music. Also, cell members who have
gained confidence through praying and participation in the cell,
may on the Sunday be far more bold, not only in singing but in
praying out loud and joining in whatever way is appropriate.

It has long been said within leadership circles that one of the
greatest challenges in church is getting the group of leaders to
worship. So one aim of the prototype cell is to get these cell
leaders and potential cell leaders to become worshippers, and
hopefully experience a new dynamic in the presence of Jesus.

3. The word.   The third 'w' is the word. This is the hardest bit to
get right, largely because what we don't want in the main cells
and also these prototype cells is a formal Bible study. What we
do want is to experience the Bible in such a way that it is not just
an intellectual exercise, but it is a spiritual encounter that challenges us to live differently. We want an environment for spiritual

growth, for every member in ministry and for honesty and accountability. Again, in the cell outlines at the end of this book we have given some suggestions for this segment of the cell.

There are three component parts to the word segment. First, there is something to understand. We want to grapple with the word of God. Second, we want to ask, 'What is its application for today?' Go round the group and ask, 'How does this principle/passage/idea impact the way we live now and in the future?' What we are hoping will take place, both in our prototype cells and in the cells we're starting in the church, is the strong encouragement to hear the members answering these questions, and not the leaders. This then achieves two things: we are taking more responsibility for our spiritual development, and we also have to engage more practically with what we are talking about. Once we have done this, we come to the third, and most exciting – but also the most difficult – part. We ask the group, 'Who needs help to see this principle/idea at work in their life?' This should definitely be asked in our prototype cells, and hopefully it will lead to one of the main leaders or potential leaders sharing a need, being honest about a problem or weakness, or perhaps even confessing a sin. The rest of the group might then want to gather around that individual, maybe by sitting them on a chair in the middle of a circle, each putting an arm on their shoulder, or whatever is appropriate, so that every member is encouraged to minister to that person's need. This ministering can mean several things: some may pray; others may read a relevant passage of Scripture; others might use a gift of the Spirit, such as a word of knowledge or a prophecy. Hopefully, by doing this, two things will happen: the person being prayed for will meet with Christ, and the people doing the ministry will have realized that God can use them.

But we don't want to leave it here. If at all possible, we want to encourage a practical outworking of this time of ministry, because in the end, cells are not a meeting; they are a community. Here's one example. I was in a cell, where a member was caring for his elderly mother at home. In the cell, the member broke down and shared how difficult this was, and how bitter he and his family sometimes felt about having to do this. He cried out loud for a new attitude and a new heart, and he was ministered to and prayed for. At the same time, the cell leader suggested that maybe one or two of the cell members could give him a day off from his mother, once a week, so that he could get a little bit of respite and relaxation.

Along this theme, in order to build community, the prototype cell leader might want to be aware if a member has a financial need and perhaps take up an offering, or encourage the cell members to meet that need practically. These are all things we want to happen in the real cells, so we definitely want to experience them in the prototype.

4. The witness. The last 'w' is the witness. This is obviously a crucial part of our cell life, as it is based on value and multiplication. Our cell is there to empower its members into relationships with non-Christians. Our hoped-for goal in the real cells is that each cell member will have at least three non-Christian friends, and that over a one- to two-year period, through friendship, through prayer and through the moving of God's Spirit, these friends will have an opportunity to experience Christ.

In our prototype cell, which only lasts for twelve weeks, we obviously cannot go through that entire cycle. But we want to at least experience some of this in terms of a new passion among us for the lost. The fact is that many of us, as leaders, are some of the most ghettoized people on the face of the earth. We hardly know any non-Christians as friends. Again, in the cell outlines at the end of this book, we have given some suggestions on what to do with this 'witness' segment.

Basically, in the three months we have given ourselves, we want to cover the following areas. First, we want to pray every week. We want to ask God what the main influences in our geographical area are that hold people back from giving their lives to Christ. And in each cell, for five to ten minutes, we want to pray hard for our general area. Hopefully this will begin to give us a sense of God's heart for the people around us. Second, in one or two of the prototype cell meetings, we want to discuss what evangelism is, and hopefully come to the understanding that it is a relational process with a non-Christian – that through our lifestyle and works, we should seek to win them to Christ. Stress that this is something that every single one of us can be involved in. Third, we want to start to make local friends. Often the friends we have at work, as good as they may be, live nowhere near us. We must continue to witness to them, but realize that this is a missionary activity as far as their attendance at a local church goes. Most likely they will not be coming to our church.

The first golden rule is that all friendships are made in the context of something else. So we want to, in the witness segment of two or three of our cell meetings, ask people to break up into small groups and think of ways they can get involved in their community. What already existing activity can they be involved in, so that through this activity they can meet non-Christian friends? Perhaps it could be joining a parent–teacher association, or a golf club and only playing with non-Christians. In the last of our prototype cell meetings, in the witness segment, we should ask people to share what they are going to do to make friends. That is as far as we can probably go within the prototype twelve-week scenario. But, hopefully, by then both the main leaders and the potential cell leaders will not be asking or challenging their cell members to do something they've not already begun to do themselves.

It is important that the leaders begin to have a passion for relational-based evangelism. It might be good for them to go through the first stage of the evangelism process, spending five weeks praying for their area, calling out to God for the town or city they live in. Then a further two to three weeks should be spent discussing what evangelism is. And another two to three weeks can be used to design a personal strategy – how they are going to make friends and find time to be involved in relational-based evangelism.

Equipping and accountability

One of the values of cell church is that every member should grow and we should all seek to be accountable. One possible way of doing this is for each leader to study some pre-set material on their own for four weeks out of the twelve. Many of the cell churches around the world are using material that is written by Ralph Neighbour, in particular a book called *The Arrival Kit*. This is an excellent resource, and is designed to bring every Christian to a basic level of maturity. It works on the basis of self-learning. Each individual is encouraged to work through the material for five days of the week, taking just 10 to 15 minutes per day. Then once a week they should meet with another cell member, an accountability partner, to share what they have learned from the material. They could also ask for help, if needed, in applying it to their life.

Church members often wonder whether their leaders ask them to do things they never do themselves. As cell leaders, we will be asking our church members to find ways to grow effectively and be accountable. If we have done this ourselves for four weeks in the prototype cell, meeting an accountability partner four times, we will be building both a practical and spiritual foundation for all that we are going to ask our church members to do.

Scared of structure

I am sure all of us want to lead meetings that are controlled by the Holy Spirit. It is my firm conviction that having a little structure, similar to the one I have outlined, does not limit the Holy Spirit. We are creating a space for God to break in, while not sticking legalistically to the structure. As the prototype cell leader, it is important to go into each of the cells having prayed beforehand and thus having some sense of what direction God would have us go in.

Create honesty

Help people to share. When it comes to the ministry time in the cell, encourage people to reach out in faith, expecting God to work through them in gifts, like prophecy or words of knowledge. We have often seen God at work in big meetings, but it is my belief that God wants to move just as mightily and powerfully in these small groups of Christians gathering together in cells. We want to see the Holy Spirit moving in our midst, not only in terms of ministering to us, but also in terms of seeing our non-Christian friends being won to Christ. We want to see God building real community with groups of Christians who love and care.

Twelve weeks is our normal guideline for a prototype cell. It might take longer. Obviously you want people to really experience cell life, honesty and community, to be a part of what is happening and then begin to see the Holy Spirit at work and lives being changed. The prototype cell is likely to be a pretty intense experience for the leaders. But if a church is going to experience a successful transition, the leaders putting the theory into practice like this will help them hugely in ensuring that the transition works.

Prototype cells for potential cell leaders

Having completed the leadership cell, the next phase would be to run another prototype cell, with potential cell leaders. If there are two or even three leaders from the initial leadership cell who feel confident to lead a prototype cell leaders' cell, you could have three prototypes running at this point. These would contain the potential cell leaders, plus their partners, if appropriate. Again, the prototype cells would last for twelve weeks. During these twelve weeks, you would want the potential cell leaders to experience much of what we have already described in the leadership cell, but with a few differences.

The main difference would be that on alternate weeks, instead of having an edification time (the third 'w', or the word), there would be some cell leader training. So the potential cell leaders are experiencing a cell for twelve weeks, and at the same time are having six periods of training. The training material could be drawn from the *Cell Leader Guidebook* by Ralph Neighbour. The subjects to be covered would include:

1. The cell leader as shepherd.
2. Stages of cell life.
3. Building community.
4. Principles of delegation and facilitating leading.
5. How to deal with various personality types within a cell.
6. How to trust God as a cell leader and know his anointing on your leadership.

The six periods of training could be backed up with a day seminar on cell leading. This seminar would need to include the theory of cell-based evangelism, the process of evangelism in the life of the cell, keys of multiplication, and also the skills and tools of cell leading.

This potential cell leaders' training cell should have no more than twelve people in it. As the cell progresses and the training develops, it will be clear who will become the main cell leaders and who should be the assistant cell leaders. Out of this group, it ought to be possible to start four to five cells. Each of these cells could potentially have ten people in them, giving you 50 church members who are now in cells. Or, if three of these prototypes were run, you would end up with up to 150 people in cells.

Another option is to have twelve weeks of prototype cell with no training for cell leadership in those twelve weeks, to make sure the cell leaders have really understood what cell is about. If the cell leaders do not really understand what a cell is, we can give them all the theoretical training we like and they might end up still leading an old house group, as they have not changed their mentality. So it might be better in some cases to do twelve weeks of cell and then another six where you put in the training, or have two or three weekends of training.

The second phase of transition

Having completed the leadership training for potential cell leaders, you are now at least six months into your transition phase. There ought to be one or two things happening during this second phase, which will affect the larger church. The leaders who have been through their leadership cell now know the theory and have experienced personally the dynamics of cell life. This would be a good time for them to begin to teach the vision and values of the process to the wider church. Also during this time, the church leaders need to finalize their overall strategy for the future of the church.

In one sense, the smaller the church is, the easier the transition process; the bigger the church, the more complicated, for obvious reasons. In a big church, more alterations may need to be made to the existing church programme, so that there are fewer activities competing with the cells. The most complex problem a larger church has to face is that when they launch their first cell they will obviously not be able to fit the whole church in. Depending on how big the church is and how many leaders they've been able to train through the prototype, it could be a one- to four-year process of placing every member in a cell. This could obviously be a little messy, as it might create an insider/outsider kind of feeling. This process definitely needs to be thought through very carefully, with a detailed strategy developed, especially for the larger church that will not be able to place every church member in a cell the first time round. For larger churches, a number of strategies have been used. It is better to go slowly through the prototype phase, your first actual cells, which will then multiply into the rest of the church. This could take a number of years. So in the meantime you may have to let some old house groups continue to run, or create a special meeting on a Wednesday night where you do some teaching and training on the seven cell values and put people into random groups based loosely on the four 'W's structure. Confusing as this may be for the larger church, it is still better to go slowly, making sure that the groups that multiply really are cell-like, and not put everybody into cells, which might cause you to have some cells that don't really operate like cells; this could result in some people not wanting to be in them at all.

The transition process   To recap the transition process thus far:

- The church leaders have thought, prayed and evaluated whether or not they want to go down the cell route.
- They have run a leadership prototype cell.
- They have run a prototype cell for potential cell leaders.
- They have begun a vision/value-sharing process with the wider church.
- They have begun to think through what this means to their existing church structures and programmes.
- If appropriate, they have thought about what they are going to do with the people who will not be part of the first roll-out of cells.
- They have begun the process of thinking about the place of children and youth in their church.

Now let us look at the next stage in the process of transition.

The third phase of transition

As the first 'real-time' cells (i.e. the permanent cells) are begun, it is important that the evaluation and encouragement process for cell leaders is happening. There are a number of things that should be in place at this transitional phase:

- Have cell co-ordinators appointed, who will meet with the cell leaders once a month.
- Have a monthly meeting, where cell leaders are encouraged with the *vision*, have an opportunity to *share* what is happening, and are given some *strategic* encouragement.
- A number of churches that went through this transition period felt that they should provide the cell leaders with a weekly

guide sheet for the first few months of the cell. A possible sheet could have an idea for the welcome section, suggestions for worship, a few points taken from the previous Sunday's message, along with appropriate questions, and a suggested activity for the witness section. On the back of the sheet you could have a weekly evaluation form for the cell leader to fill in. This form can become a personal diary for the cell leader so they can remember what has happened in the cell. The forms can then be shared with the cell co-ordinator when they meet on a monthly basis. The evaluation form could be like the one worked out by Andy Read at the River Church. It has five sections:

1. Which group members were asked to lead the different sections of the meeting? (Have you given them any feedback to encourage them?)
2. Noteworthy information from ice-breaker time.
3. Issues raised in the meeting (especially the word section) that need following up.
4. Which people need to be prayed for this week?
5. Overall feeling about the meeting.

As we have seen, one of the major problems that transition could bring up is what to do with the people who are not able to get into cells. There are a number of ways that this can be dealt with: the existing house-group system could be continued, running alongside the new cells; or perhaps a Wednesday night meeting could be held, where some of the values and vision of cell church could be taught. Then people could be broken up into temporary cells, all of them running on the four 'W's system. Even though these will not be real cells, they will begin to give people the idea of what being in a real cell might be like.

The second pathway: the 'big bang'

We have looked in some detail at transition using the prototype model, but the other possibility is to do what is sometimes called 'transition by the big bang'. In other words, cell leaders are trained as quickly as possible and everybody is put into cells.

Now this is a very real possibility, and it sometimes appears to be the best route for a number of reasons: it is quick; you might be able to train enough cell leaders to get everybody into cells, and when you're excited about the vision of cell church, waiting six months before you have your first real roll-out of cells seems a very long time.

However, the experience of many churches that have tried this process is that some of the potential cell leaders still have an old model in their head. Therefore, the new cells look very much like old house groups. Having built up everybody's expectations through sharing the vision and values, you then have to cope with the negativity that is raised by cells that are not really working. Obviously there is the chance that cells won't work in the proto-type system as well, but because the cell leaders have actually experienced being in a cell for three months, they should have got a real picture of what it is like. So, hopefully, there will be fewer leaders running the cells on the old house-group model. The other drawback of the big bang is that it is perhaps too quick a process for the church. They will not have had enough time to think through the value changes. This particularly relates to some of the key values: is there an environment for honesty where people will begin to open up their lives, and is there a real commitment to network relational evangelism?

Having been slightly negative about this approach, I will admit that there are situations where it would be suitable, particularly in small churches. But perhaps the right way would be to follow the first pathway, but cut out the leadership cell prototype and go straight to the leadership training prototype.

Real-time cells

Whether your transition is the prototype or the big bang version, eventually you will come to the first real-time cells. These cells should last at least a year, and you will have two choices to make regarding them. One is that you leave them until they multiply through evangelism only. In that sense it will be a real-time cell. The second option is that if you still have other church members who need to be put into cells, you could multiply your cells with church members. In a sense it would not be a real-time cell, but if it is run for a year, people will have had a genuine experience of cell life, and they will have gone through most of an evangelism cycle. They may even have led one or two people to Christ.

Conclusion

Bill Beckham offers the following list, which underlines the areas we need to look at in terms of the overall transition:

- Groups – change from a multi-group system into a primary cell system with sub-groups.
- Bible study – change from an information-based teaching system into an application-based learning system.
- Equipping – change from an optional teacher system for new believers into required personal growth in cells.
- Learning – change from a teaching approach of gradualism into an intensive encounter learning system.

- Ministry – change from staff-driven ministry to member-driven ministry.
- Evangelism – change from 'vacuum cleaner' church growth into relationship-based cell evangelism.
- Accountability – change from primarily doctrinal accountability into community-centred mutual support.
- Youth – change from an activities-driven youth programme into a cell community preparation system.
- Children – change from a cognitive school-type programme for children into family community relationships.
- Leadership – change from a narrow 'professional' staff system into a broad-based multi-level approach.
- Administration – change from a compartmentalized administrative system into an integrated administrative system.

Summary

- The process of changing the church into the cell model follows the sequence:

Beliefs → Vision → Values → Transition of
structures → Cell church.

- The leaders follow this path and then allow the church at large an opportunity to adjust its beliefs and values before the structural changes take place.
- Steps to transition are:
  1. Preach and teach the understanding about church and everyone playing their part.
  2. Explore together the values that uphold cell church.
  3. Strategy for changing structures:

- Prototype cells for church leaders and potential cell leaders.
- Teach the vision and values to the whole church.
- Plan to change the existing structures and programmes.
- Plan for the children and youth.
- Begin the first 'real-time' cells by folding church members into the prototype or by releasing the trained cell leaders to form cells.
- Appoint cell co-ordinators from the leadership team.
- Establish the cell leaders' meeting.

5

The Internal Structure of a Cell Meeting

One of the ways cells differ from house groups is that they have an internal structure. The structure enables the values that the cells are built on to take place. Some people may be excited about the possibility of an internal structure within the cells. Others could feel this is an imposition. Let me put your mind at rest.

There are a number of possible structures that are used around the world, but they are not designed to be legalistic. They are a guide to the facilitator leader, so that the cell really supports and encourages the members as they live out the values we have looked at, instead of becoming a group that is leader dominated, a social chat point, or a holy huddle. The structure we shall highlight here was developed by Ralph Neighbour and Bill Beckham, and is based on the four 'W's, which stand for: welcome, worship, word and witness (see Chapter 4). If the cell has a structure like this, there are a number of important things you can do. First, you can train cell leaders. In the past, when a group has had its own often undefined set of values and its own ideas about how it should operate, it has been very difficult to train a leader specifically for the group. Having a clear structure enables dynamic training to take place, as the facilitator leader can be taught the skills they will need in order to run their cell. A cell co-ordinator can meet with the cell leader on a regular basis, observe the cell and see how it is working according to the values and structure. Second, it will be easier to evaluate the group if there are agreed values and structures. Third, clearly defined values and structures enable less experienced Christians to become cell leaders. Young people and relatively new Christians can lead the meetings because their task is well defined and achievable.

Let us look at this internal structure in more detail. First, the welcome section.

Welcome

Two of the values in the cell system are 'every member in ministry' and 'honesty'. In the welcome section, once people have sat down and had a cup of tea or coffee, the cell leader should ask everybody a simple, open question. It could be a question like: 'What was your favourite music between the ages of 14 and 18, and how did it influence you?' At the beginning of the cell cycle, as the group is forming, these questions will be quite light. As the cell develops, they may become more personal, such as: 'Which person most influenced you between the ages of 14 and 18, and why?'; 'What do you most like about yourself?', or 'When did God become more than a word to you?'

This initial welcome achieves two things. First, once everybody has spoken, there is nobody in the group who is a spectator; everyone has become a participator, and they are given significance as the rest of the group listens without interruption to their answer. Second, community begins. Real community between people begins with the interchange of information and the acceptance that results from this. Week by week, as members of the group share things about themselves – sometimes even trivial things – community is being created. This is an important cell value.

Another value of cell church is honesty. We cannot expect, and neither should we, that people are going to share their life problems and intimate details in the first few cell meetings. It will take a number of months for trust to develop. But as people are honest with what could be called the superficial details of life, this builds an atmosphere where really significant things can be shared in the future. Having said this, it is the experience of many cell churches that even when people answer relatively superficial questions, the acceptance they feel and the fact that they are being listened to has a profound effect right from the beginning. Often, in existing house groups, you can be a member for many years and know very little about the people in your group. But the welcome part of the cell meeting – lasting 15 to 20 minutes in the early days of the cell, and maybe a little less later on – brings a radical transformation in people's participation and knowledge of each another.

It is common for cell and church leaders to underestimate the impact of this person-to-person part of the meeting. Many cell churches can testify how this simple act of participative welcome has revolutionized their cell. It is the favourite section of many cell members.

Worship

The second major section of the cell meeting is the worship. This is obviously linked to the value of Jesus being at the core of the cell. Jesus said, 'For where two or three come together in my name, there am I with them' (Matthew 18:20). In the end, it is only Jesus who can really change us – not having good cell meetings or great structures. The heart of Christianity is our personal and corporate relationship with Jesus. It is his presence within the cell that in the end brings profound changes in people's personal lives. It is his presence that inspires us not to keep his love for ourselves but to reach out to a wider world.

The worship section, which again could last 15 to 20 minutes, does not have to include music. Some of the most embarrassing experiences of people's lives have taken place in times of singing in small groups where there are one or two people who are about as musical as a brick. One of the gifts that God has given his people is creativity. During the life of our cell we can experience worship in many different ways, including non-musical. For example, the person leading this segment could read out John 3:16: 'For God so loved the world that he gave his one and only Son, that whoever believes in him shall not perish but have eternal life.' He or she could then ask each cell member to reflect on this passage for two minutes, and then share something from it that has spoken to them. In one cell where this was done, a person called John shared how it had struck him that God really loved him. Someone else shared how they realized that God's love is not abstract – he really made a sacrifice. Maybe not everyone will say something, but over a few minutes different thoughts will be shared. These can be turned into prayers, with, for example: 'Let us thank God for what he has done for us.' This may be followed by a time of thanksgiving.

All of this may take 15 minutes, and at the end of the segment a genuine act of worship will have taken place. There are hundreds of creative ideas that could be used as simple acts of non-musical worship, as well as many ways we can worship God through music, with or without a musician. For example, a tape of Christian music could be played, and there could follow a private personal response, or just a time of thanking God for who he is, or people could reflect on what the song said to them.

Word

The third 'W' is the word section. The values that relate to this section are honesty, every member in ministry (as people pray and care for one another practically), and Jesus at the centre (as they experience the love of God in the ministry). Whereas in the traditional house group there might have been a Bible study with one person speaking, sharing what they thought the Scriptures might be saying, in the cell, we want people to encounter the word and apply it to their lives.

It could work like this. What was taught on Sunday in the larger meeting could become the foundation for discussion and application in the cell. This may present a number of challenges. First of all, what is taught in the larger gathering needs to be worth discussing. I am sure many of us have been to meetings on Sunday where the sermon wasn't worth discussing at the coffee time at the end, let alone on Wednesday night.

Ideally, the person who prepares the Sunday message should also provide two or three questions for discussion in the cell. These questions can relate to two basic themes: 1. What did the speaker say and what do we understand about it? 2. How can we apply what was said to our lives? The second question should lead to a vital part of the word segment – a time of personal ministry. The cell leader could ask a question like: 'Who needs help to apply this to their life?' There will then be an opportunity for the cell to minister to one another.

If someone has indicated they need help, perhaps they could sit on a chair in the middle. It is important that the cell leader emphasizes that this is the cell members ministering to one another, and that, from the youngest to the most mature, they can all take part. People could be encouraged to read a scripture for the person they are ministering to, share some wisdom, or they could move out into the gifts of the Spirit, such as speaking out a prophecy or a word of knowledge.

Just as an aside here, one of the recent challenges of the charismatic movement has been that it is not very charismatic. Michael (not his real name), a well-known leader of a dynamic missionary organization that was renowned for being charismatic, was approached by a staff member, who asked him: 'Why aren't we as charismatic as we used to be?' Michael, in good fashion, dealt with this unruly staff member by explaining that their organization was just as charismatic as it had ever been. As he walked away from this encounter, feeling somewhat smug, he suddenly felt the Holy Spirit whispering to him, 'Michael, why is your organization not as charismatic as it once was?' Naturally, Michael found it one thing to argue with a staff member, but quite another to take on the Holy Spirit. He began to realize that what the staff member had said was in fact true. As the organization had grown, big meetings became more important, and as the big meetings became more important, slowly but surely there was less room for people to move in the gifts of the Spirit.

The fact is that in big meetings, three groups of people will move in the gifts: leaders, extroverts and quirky people. The ordinary church member who may sense something from God would probably need a handwritten invitation by God himself, presented by an angel, to get out of their chair in a big meeting! Cells, however, provide a whole new opportunity to see the Holy

Spirit at work. In the small group, in a non-threatening situation, with a leader present, you have the perfect environment for people to be encouraged to share. Through the time of ministry in your cell, individual cell members can meet with Jesus. The other cell members will go away encouraged, feeling that God can use them. If this type of ministry happens in a cell, there won't be any difficulty persuading people to come the following week. There is a longing in many people's heart to meet with Jesus. By the word of God becoming alive and practical, and not just some theoretical principle, we can see God build his body, with those who are ministered to and those who minister.

In summary, there are three aspects to the word section. First, there is something to understand, whether this is gleaned from what was taught on Sunday, or something the cell has explored together, which may have been prepared by a cell member or leader. Second: How does this apply to my life today? How does it impact my actions and my values? Third: Who needs help? At this point, as already explained, people will be encouraged to respond with prayer and practical support.

Witness

Now we move on to the last 'W': the witness section. In a later chapter, we will go into this in more detail. As is the conviction of many who have been working in the cell movement, this is going to be the most challenging area for us. The other three areas are definitely things God has been working on in the churches in the last 20 years.

So what is the witness section? What is cell-based evangelism? Perhaps we should start with what it is not. It is not about the cell going out as a whole, standing on street corners and preaching.

It is not about bringing every non-Christian acquaintance into the cell. It is about empowering each cell member to climb out of their Christian ghetto and into their local environment to make unchurched friends. These are genuine friendships, not just acquaintances for their converting potential. But obviously, as Christians love people, these people might hear, see and experience Jesus. So, during the cycle of the cell, the cell will help each person make friends, local friends. They will then pray for those friends. It might be the goal of the cell for each cell member to make three unchurched friends. If the cell, over a period of time, has 30 unchurched friends, it is the hope and prayer of this cell that over the one- to two-year cycle, five of them will come to Christ. This will be enough to multiply the cell. This may sound a lot easier than it really is, and we will consider it in detail in Chapter 7.

The cell will also recognize the ways we can love the lost. Matthew 5:13–16 encourages us to be salt and light in the world. Also, 1 John 3:8 says that the Son of man came to destroy the works of the devil: 'The reason the Son of God appeared was to destroy the devil's work.' The body of Christ needs to infiltrate society at a local and national level, to be salt and light – to express the love of Christ in our actions, in caring for the poor and needy, and in every sphere, be it the market-place, the media, arts, government, or wherever, in order to bring about Christian values and principles. This sphere of salt and light has not been a strong area of emphasis for churches, particularly in the last 20 years. Much of our thinking has been about the local environment. And yet within our churches, the majority of our congregations are involved in their own market-place from Monday to Friday, 7am to 7pm. These individuals are often confused about their Christianity in this context. They feel under-encouraged and under-mobilized. They just about understand what they ought to be doing in terms of local church and local community, but no one has told them what they could be doing with this salt and light mandate in the rest of their lives.

We have all heard the horror stories – here's a typical example. One bright lawyer called Peter has a terrific opportunity to influence the city of London. But he is told by his pastor that if he really loved God he wouldn't be doing what he is doing. Instead, he should give more time to his local church. What a waste! Whether people are working as secretaries, lawyers, nurses, artists or bricklayers, they all have something to say. So the cell, in its witness section, needs, over a few weeks, to work its way round its cell members. Perhaps Jenny is a nurse in your cell. Jenny could be asked what it means to be a Christian nurse today: 'What ethical and moral struggles do you face in your job? How can you be salt and light in the workplace?' Jenny could then be encouraged in her salt and light mandate. Or perhaps Jim, an architect, who works for the prison service and helps to set the national parameters in terms of designing prison cells and prisons, needs encouragement. He might be desperate for people to say to him: 'If Jesus were designing a prison, what would it look like?' How can he bring his Christian morality and world-view into his office on a Monday morning? Jim has a crucial opportunity to be salt and light, yet perhaps never in his Christian experience has anybody ever spoken to him about this, encouraged or empowered him.

It is time for the body of Christ to be mobilized. It is time for us to make a difference, in terms of winning people for Christ, and in terms of touching our nation – but it will only happen if we hold one another accountable for the gifts and opportunities God has given us, and if we empower each other through the pressures and strains of putting it into practice. This is cell life. This is the body of Christ.

Structure

We must have a realistic view of the internal structure of the four 'W's that we are seeking to carry out on a week-by-week basis. The structure is a guide; it is not set in stone. In the life of the cell, the amount of time spent on the various sections might change.

In the first three months of the cell, we might spend a lot more time on the first two 'W's, in terms of getting to know one another and building community. During the next six months, we might spend more time on the word segment, building one another up. Then, in the following nine months, we might focus more on the witness section, reaching out to our friends and building a strategy to multiply the cell. It is the role of the cell co-ordinator to ensure the cell doesn't swerve to any particular emphasis, so that over the life of the cell there is a balance between the four 'W's. We will look into this a bit further in Chapter 8.

So what will the cell meeting actually be like? First, the cell will probably decide for itself when it will meet, with some guidance from the wider church. If it is a purely adult cell, it is probably going to meet in an evening. It will try to meet in different cell members' houses, so that any parents can be involved without having to worry about babysitters. There should be flexibility with regard to time and place, but the cell will probably gather together, have a tea or coffee, and then start the meeting.

There are two models to leading the cell: one is that the cell is always facilitated by the cell leader, and assistant cell leader, and they lead all the segments; the second is that after an initial period of time, there is a delegating process to cell members. There are strengths and weaknesses in both of these models. After the first few cell meetings, the cell leader will hopefully delegate aspects of the meeting to different cell members. So somebody will do the welcome, somebody else might do the word, and the cell leader could do the witness. Responsibilities for segments can be swapped around on a week-by-week basis. Or it might be that you ask someone to do four or five welcome or worship sections in a row so that, as the cell leader, you can encourage, train and help them. This way they can learn how to lead their particular segment more dynamically.

Remember, this is only a guide; the cell leader may have to show sensitivity and be flexible. Maybe in the welcome you have gone round and asked the question: 'What do you most like about yourself?' One of the cell members might have said, 'Could I just have a moment to think about this?' So the question would have gone round the cell, and everybody would have shared. Meanwhile, this person would have sat very quietly with two large tears forming in their eyes as they said to the cell, 'I don't like anything about myself.' This is not the time for the cell leader to say, 'Now let's move on to the worship section.' The leader should sensitively take the opportunity to say to this person, 'Do you mind if we pray for you?' Then the cell can minister in whatever way is appropriate. Another example would be if, in the middle of a worship time, the presence of God turns up in a powerful way. Right at the most sensitive moment, the cell leader should not look at his or her watch and say, 'Right, we've done this for 15 minutes; it's time to move on now.' Obviously they would roll with that time of worship and let it run on. It might be that in that particular meeting you don't get to the witness section. It might be that the ministry time in the word section also runs on. This is fine. However, if over a period of weeks you never have a word section because the worship runs over every time – or if you never have a witness section because the word runs on – this is obviously not good. The cell leader needs to ensure that this is not the case.

The underlying principle is that we want to see people blessed so that they can be a blessing, and face their responsibility of being salt and light. The structure is a framework, or a guide. It is not a legalistic structure, with 15 minutes of this, 15 of that, and 10 of this. In the hands of a good cell leader, the cell may not even know that there is a framework to the meetings.

Summary

- The internal structure of the cell enables:
  1. Effective training of cell leaders.
  2. Effective evaluation of the progress of the cell.
  3. Less experienced believers to become cell leaders.
- The four 'W's:
  1. Welcome:
     - Begins to form community by the sharing of information by all the cell members.
     - The commitment to honesty and trust is facilitated.
     - The potential for every member to participate in ministry is released by ensuring that every member makes a contribution.
  2. Worship:
     - Encourages the group to let Jesus be at the centre of the lives of the individuals and of the cell group.

3. Word:
  - Cell members encounter the word of God with an expectation to apply what they learn to their lives.
  - Cell members are encouraged to mature and are helped by the ministry of others in the group.
4. Witness:
  - Cell members learn to be motivated out of God's heart for those who don't know him.
  - They are empowered to make real friendships with unbelievers, to consistently pray for them and those things that hold them back from believing.
  - The cell works together to build relationships with each other's friends, to see some come to know Jesus.
  - Cell members are also supported in being salt and light in their workplace and communities.
- The structure
  - Supports the values, but is flexible so that there can be a response to God's agenda for each meeting.

6

The Cell Leader and the Skills for Leading Cells

It would be true to say that a cell church is only as good as the cells within it. The role of the cell leader is key in enabling healthy cell life on a week-by-week, month-by-month basis. In churches with house groups, the house-group leader has often been under-trained, under-encouraged and left on their own. In contrast to this, the cell leader needs to be trained, encouraged and not left on their own. As cell church grows, so does our need for good cell leaders.

So what are the characteristics of a good cell leader, and what training do they need?

Values

Let us go back to cell values for a moment. As in any appointment or structural change, these values need to influence us. There are three key values here that will impact who we choose to be cell leaders, and how exactly we train them.

1. Jesus

First of all, cells are about Jesus, so we need cell leaders who have a simple passion for Christ. They don't have to be the most educated or talented people, but they do need to love Jesus. Perhaps there are three characteristics of their love for Jesus that we ought to look out for. One is teachability – that if we love Jesus, we are open to God to keep working on us as an individual. Second, we are not so defensive towards others, and we have an attitude to learn, which is going to be very important for any cell leader. Third, as a part of our love for Jesus, we have a growing concern and passion for the lost. This does not mean every cell leader and potential cell leader needs to be a raving evangelist, but they need to have some passion to touch their neighbourhood to see the lost saved.

2. Every member in ministry

Another key value is every member in ministry, so we are looking for a different sort of leader. This person is often called a facilitator leader – someone who has a heart not to dominate or do everything, but to make room, to encourage, and draw out what is hidden in other people's lives. We are probably looking for people who are relational. They may not necessarily be the best Bible teachers or the strongest personalities, even though these are the people we might have used in the old system.

3. Honesty

The third key value we should consider is honesty. In the end, people follow leaders, so we want to have cell leaders who are an example in everything they do. We want people who can create a culture of honesty, are honest, who can share their weaknesses

and are prepared to be real. The stereotype of Christian leadership is that the leader never shares his or her weaknesses, remains
strong and can always 'make it' in the Christian life. There is
sometimes the fear that we will lose respect if we share faults and
weaknesses in our lives, but this is far from the truth. The reality
is that when we are weak and vulnerable in front of people, it
actually builds respect.

These three values tell us a little bit about the type of person we
are looking for to be a cell leader: someone who has a heart for
Jesus, a passion for others and is honest. However, they still need
to be a leader. Even if he or she leads through a facilitating style,
they need to have confidence, and those who appoint them need
to have confidence that they can lead.

   On top of this, it is to be hoped that the cell leader will have
experienced what a cell is really like, either through a prototype
cell or their own cell. If they have not experienced a cell, there is
a real danger that they will model their cell on what other small
group experiences they have had. This will not be helpful.

Leading is easy

How difficult is it to lead a cell? As we choose our prospective cell
leaders and start to train them, we need to sense what level of
maturity and leadership they might require. This might not be a
problem when we begin our cells. We may have in our church a
pool of existing leaders, and people who do have the potential to
be good assistant leaders who will then be able to lead themselves. In the not too distant future, though, as cells begin to
multiply, we are going to have to release into leadership a whole
group of people who might never have had this opportunity. As

we look at the role and tasks of a cell leader, we need to be careful we don't make things too complex, otherwise we will find it impossible to multiply ourselves, as we won't have enough suitable leaders.

This is one of the major reasons we use an internal structure like the four 'W's. The structure automatically gives the cell leader a clear idea what they need to do on a meeting-by-meeting basis. Early on they will also be delegating various aspects of the four 'W's. Having an internal structure like this, and the motivation to facilitate, makes cell leading a lot easier. Given 90 minutes to fill with no clear structure, even experienced leaders will find cell leading quite difficult. By having a dynamic structure and clear expectations, we have probably made the job half as difficult as it might have been.

Also, the cell leader will have a cell co-ordinator (explained at length in Chapter 8), who hopefully will sit in their cell on a once-a-month basis and also meet with them personally. This should help them a great deal. With the supervisor there to hold the hand of the cell leader (metaphorically speaking), the job should be simpler still. Which brings up another thing to bear in mind as we appoint our cell leaders: they need to be people who accept advice and won't feel threatened by a person who is over them. In the first cell they lead, and especially in the first six months, they might get a lot of advice and input from the cell co-ordinator.

The tasks of a leader

As you can see, leading a cell need not be a huge responsibility, and it is in the grasp of many mature believers. So what are the tasks of the cell leader? Here are a few:

- To lead through facilitating the involvement and ministry of each cell member.
- To initially organize the practicalities of coming together: when and where the cell is going to meet, and drawing together the various cell members, through whatever system the church decides.
- To lead the cell meeting on a weekly basis, basing it on the four 'W's but remembering that it is a dynamic process. Also, as soon as possible delegating various segments of the cell to assistant cell leaders and other cell members.
- To facilitate community in the cell group.
- To facilitate the pastoral welfare of each cell member.

Facilitating community

Cell life is not about cell meetings; it is about a group of people being church and Christian family together. In the early stages of the cell, a vital part of the cell leader's role is to make sure this happens. How can they begin to facilitate community? First, they need to know all of their cell members. Second, through meetings and social events, they need to encourage the cell members to get to know one another, if they don't already. The cell meeting is the focus of the community, but real community development requires contact outside the weekly meeting.

Many cell churches use a tool devised by Ralph Neighbour, called a Journey Guide. This has been developed into a book, but it started life as a questionnaire. As the cell leader goes through it individually with each cell member, they will find out a great deal about that person's background, spiritual experience and possible strongholds in their lives. In general terms, they will have a clear assessment of the different maturity levels of their cell members. This should be done in an informal, chatty way in the person's home. As you may know, a great deal can be learned about a person by visiting them in their home environment.

Another way of facilitating community is to allow plenty of time for the welcome section in the early stages of the cell. People will slowly find out about each other and begin to enter into each other's lives. As they sacrificially love each other, community will begin to form.

Pastoral responsibility

Another major task of the cell leader is to facilitate the pastoral welfare of each cell member. Again, there are some important aspects of cell church to think about here. Even though the cell leader is taking some responsibility for the cell members, the leader is not expected to do all the pastoring and caring. It is to be hoped that the cell itself, in a sense, will care for itself – that in the word section, as people are open and share their needs, they will be prayed for and cared for by other cell members. As individuals meet with Jesus in the context of the cell, they will be empowered and pastored. Also, in many cell churches, there is often a relationship of mutual care between individual cell members – where a mature cell member meets on a regular basis with another cell member to work through teaching material with them, to pray with them and to encourage them.

Obviously there will also be times when the cell leader meets with individuals, and he or she will want to help their cell members as much as they can. However, it is important at this point that the cell leader knows what resources they have for difficult pastoral problems. If we are seeing cells multiply and are calling on lots of different people to be cell leaders, some of them will naturally have only limited pastoring skills. Therefore, there needs to be a clear referral and help system for the cell leader. Maybe they could get in touch with their cell co-ordinator and say: 'The marriage of Mr and Mrs Y seems to be in trouble, and Jane has some deep spiritual bondage in her life and I don't know what to do.' (Or whatever the case may be.) The cell co-ordinator may then take over the counselling of the cell members concerned, or refer them to a counselling or pastoral care structure that the church has. That way, the pastoral responsibility of the cell members is lifted off the cell leader for a period of time. When the cell members have got through their difficulty, the cell leader can take responsibility once again.

Assistant cell leaders

An important role of the cell leader is to develop the assistant cell leader. But one of the tasks of the cell leader is to identify someone who can be the assistant cell leader and who, by the time the cell multiplies, will be ready to lead their own cell. This may be one to two years away, so the cell leader has plenty of time to develop that person. If there isn't an obvious person in the group, in the first few months of the cell the leader might be looking at cell members and thinking and praying about who should be the assistant cell leader. Then there can be an identifying and appointing process which should be done in consultation with a cell co-ordinator. Over the next few months, the leader will slowly increase the responsibility and tasks that the assistant cell leader will have. Perhaps this will reach the point where, in the last few months of the cell before multiplication, the assistant cell leader is doing the leading and the cell leader is coaching and observing. Another of the cell leader's roles, then, is to mentor and encourage the assistant cell leader, who should also receive formal training from the church leaders.

The stages of the cell

One of the most important tasks that will begin to develop after about six months of the cell is making sure that the multiplication process is at work. So the first few months of the cell will be about building community in the cell.

The cell will go through some clear cycles. First of all, it will have what can be called the forming stage, which can be quite exciting – getting to know one another, and the buzz and excitement of a new thing starting. Then there will be the storming stage, where people will have begun to know one another. Maybe there will be comments like: 'Why is so and so in my cell?' and 'Why can't I be somewhere else?' Then, through sacrificial love and much prayer and care, the cell will enter into the normal stage where the group has fully established itself. Lastly, it will go into the stage where people are beginning to develop their ministry. They are also looking, as a cell, towards multiplication.

After the first six months, the leader needs to make sure that the fourth 'W' and the evangelism strategy as outlined in Chapter 3 is put into action. It is very important that the cell leader does not lose touch with the multiplication strategy. It is so easy to fall into the trap of being blessed, ministering to one another, and having a great time being family together, but losing sight of the fact that the cells are about pastoring and evangelism. The cell must empower each individual member into relationships with the unchurched, and have a clear strategy through the life of the cell on how they are going to pray for and win their unchurched friends.

Cell leaders' meetings

Now we have seen some of the clear tasks of the cell leader. To help them with these tasks, there will probably be other meetings they will need to attend. For example, meeting with their cell co-ordinator on a monthly basis, attending a monthly cell leaders' meeting, and to have time on an informal basis to encourage and mentor their assistant cell leader.

With this in mind, it is important to note that we do not want to develop all sorts of structures so that being a cell leader means you have no time for your family, yourself and your own responsibility for reaching your unchurched friends. It is to be hoped that the cell leaders' responsibilities could on average be contained within two nights a week. This should leave them with enough time for work, family, unchurched friends and so on.

Skills of leading cells

The cell leader should have a certain number of skills, and these skills need to be passed on to assistant cell leaders and those leading a segment of the cell.

1. Be prepared

First of all, let us look at the preparation needed for your actual cell meeting. There are two words that could best sum it up: 'prepare' and 'trust'.

Hopefully, cell leaders will have access to resources in terms of creative ideas for the welcome and worship sections. (In a later chapter, we will give ideas for the witness section.)

As far as the word section is concerned, there are two approaches that can be taken. One is that this segment can be based on what was taught in the Sunday meeting/celebration/gathering of cells. Hopefully, the Sunday speaker will supply some questions for the cell groups to work on. These questions need to cover the following: Do people understand what the material covered? How can it be applied to our lives? Who needs help, prayer and encouragement in applying it?

There are two primary ways that cell leaders can operate, both of which are happening in cell churches at the moment. One is that the cell leader, in the style of a facilitator, runs every segment of the meeting and then slowly delegates segments to the assistant cell leader and obviously, because it is a style of facilitation, cell members are contributing all the time, but the leadership remains with the cell leader and cell assistant. The second model, and the one that is described at length here, is where the cell leader will still train up the assistant leader, but will also delegate some of the segments to cell members. In the early days of the cell, for the first six or seven meetings, the cell leader may lead most of the segments himself or herself before starting to delegate them. Once the leader starts to delegate, it is important for them to communicate the purpose of each 'W' to coach the cell member in the way to do it, and to make sure those people have been given a clear time frame for their segment. If God is really moving in their segment and they want it to roll on, they need to be briefed clearly beforehand to gain eye contact with you and get the nod to continue. This is because it is very easy for someone leading a segment to get caught up in it and lose their objectivity.

If there is no material available from the Sunday talk and the cell leader needs to prepare the word section, remember that we are not trying to turn this into a Bible study, but to raise an issue, talk it through together and conclude with a form of ministry. For example, they could work through Psalm 46 and talk about trouble. They might want to open the time by saying that trouble is something we all face, and the cell could come up with some common principles from the psalm that they can all use when they face trouble. So, read the psalm verse by verse, with each member reading a verse aloud. Then give the cell members a few minutes to think about the words they have heard, asking the question, 'What principles does this psalm give to help us in times of trouble?' Next, have different members share any insights they might have. Write their thoughts down on a piece of paper. The cell leader must feel free to contribute their own thoughts as a part of the process, and hopefully will end up with a list of five or six points drawn from the psalm. Suggest to the cell that someone types these points out, so that each member can put them in their Bible and refer to them when they have a problem. Read the principles out, and ask if any cell member has ever been in trouble and one of these principles has worked for them. This way the cell leader is looking for a positive story of someone who has used one of the principles to help them overcome difficulties. This shows that the principles do work, and it helps anyone in trouble see that perhaps there is hope for them. In the process, we also find out more about each other.

In the final part of the word section, having heard a testimony or two, the leader could ask if there is anyone in the cell who is in trouble right now and doesn't know what to do. Maybe they are unemployed and are struggling financially, or have some sort of emotional struggle. If a cell member opens up, give them time to share their trouble with the group. Find an appropriate way to minister to them and have everybody pray for them. The cell leader can then encourage people to minister to that person by sharing a scripture or a piece of advice that might be relevant, or by using the gifts of the Spirit.

Having prepared for the cell meeting, the important thing to remember is 'trust'. Trust that God will step into the meeting, and that all the cell leader is called to be is faithful. It is not their job to run a successful cell meeting; it is their job to be faithful and trust that God will make that meeting a success. What does trust mean for a cell leader? For one it means praying, spending a few moments before the meeting asking that Jesus would be the centre of the cell, submitting in prayer every person who is involved, and praying that each person would meet with Jesus in some way or other. Having prayed, it is very important for the cell leader to have confidence that God will be present at the meeting. This confidence is not dependent on how the leader feels, but on the fact that God has called them to lead this cell, that they have entrusted it to God and that he will be faithful.

For example, Bob, a young cell leader, is about to lead his cell meeting, and he is very aware that his own spiritual life is going through a bit of a struggle. He rings up his assistant cell leader to see if they could take on more responsibility that evening, but they too are feeling a little out of sorts. So Bob is honest with God before the meeting. He cries out to him for help, and goes to the meeting at a pretty low ebb. He starts to lead from what he has prepared, and much to his amazement, this is the best cell meeting he has ever had. God shows up in many different ways, and individual cell members are ministered to. This is the faithfulness of God.

It is important for us to understand in all leadership that God's

anointing comes in two areas: there is an anointing on the job we
are called to do; and we also have an anointing upon our character as a follower of Jesus. If you can imagine these areas of
anointing as two horizontal lines, we want to keep those lines
running parallel. But the truth is that every now and again, we
will experience a character blip while we are in leadership. We
may have an argument with our spouse, shout at the children, or
generally just be going through a hard time. When these situations hit us, we need to understand that the anointing of appointing will still be there for us. We can go into these meetings with
confidence, provided we have done all we can to get the situation
right, and trust that God will be as much there then as in the
times when we feel we could take over the whole world single-
handedly. This is no excuse for us to sin and take the grace of
God for granted. If we carry on relying on the anointing of
appointing, but are not seeking to get our character sorted, then
at some point God will lift the anointing off the appointing and
we will be in trouble.

2. Delegate

When it comes to the meeting itself, there are a number of skills
that are useful in leading a cell, particularly if we are seeking to
facilitate others into ministry. There will follow a list of these
skills, not necessarily written in their order of importance, with
a brief description after each. But first of all we need to look at
delegation.

The idea is that the cell leaders themselves will initially lead
most of the four 'W's while the cell is being established, then after
a few weeks delegate the sections to different cell members,
perhaps keeping the word section for themselves. Ideally, the cell
leader would ask someone to do a segment for a month or six

weeks, and as the leader does that it is good if they can enter into a contract with the person being delegated to, asking if they would mind the cell leader giving regular feedback to them. That way, the cell leader will be imparting skills to specific cell members over a period of time.

3. Creating an atmosphere

There are three atmospheres we want to create within our cells. By atmosphere, we are talking about the environment that we as the leaders create, and out of this environment the cell operates. First, we want to create an environment of faith – faith that Jesus really is in the centre, that when we meet together it is not just ten people gathered in a room praying and worshipping, but these ten people have the greatest privilege that anyone in the world could possibly experience: they have gathered in the presence of Jesus Christ; God himself is in their midst, and through the life of their cell and all that takes place, each individual is going to meet with God and be changed. Be warned, though – this understanding probably won't happen in the first cell meeting. We need to create realistic expectations.

Second, we want to create an environment of safety. The cell needs to be a safe place, where people won't be shot down if they make mistakes. If anyone shares something personal, they need to have confidence that it will not be spread around the church. It would be good for the cell leader to remind people of this at the beginning of each cell cycle.

Third, we want to create an atmosphere of openness and vulnerability. Cells work best when people share what is really going on in their lives. Obviously, this will be a process – to start with, people might share quite superficial things until they begin to feel safe.

4. Ownership

It is very important that the cell leader and any contributor talks in 'we' and 'our' terms, and not 'this is my cell'. One of the major underlying values of cell church is every person in ministry, and we are seeking for the whole cell to minister together. One way for the cell leader to create a sense of common ownership is by suggesting that the cell members themselves create a list of principles that will help them when the cell goes through difficulties, or to come up with their own particular prayer strategy for one another. The important thing is that this is something the cell has worked on together – it is not an imposed idea. Another aspect of ownership is creating cell vision. In the early days the cell leader would be well advised to say why they're meeting, so that the whole vision of the cell slowly, week by week, grows as a concept in the hearts of the cell members.

5. Affirmation at all times

One of the staggering discoveries about British people, and it is perhaps true of other nationalities as well, is that the average person has a very low picture of their own self-worth. Britain is plagued with people feeling inadequate and assuming that their contribution is going to be stupid and worthless. But the fact is that when people do contribute, often it is staggering and wonderful. With this in mind, when anyone says anything or makes a contribution, the cell leader needs to make a habit of saying something to the effect of: 'That's great. Thanks for sharing that.' At all times we need to emphasize the ethos that we are here to minister and help one another in the good times and bad. When individuals contribute to any section of the cell, let's hear those mutterings of: 'Hey, that's great. Thanks for what you said.'

If people feel affirmed, they will contribute. Even if their contribution is weak, it is still their contribution and they need affirmation. And even if their contribution is wrong or bad, try not to contradict them publicly. If, in extreme situations, their contribution is out of order, it might be right to step in and say, 'Thank you for your contribution. However, that is not how I see that particular issue or subject. I see it this way.' This is so the cell knows you don't agree with that particular heresy or whatever it was. But if at all possible, avoid the public confrontation and see people privately if you are worried about something they contributed.

6. Explanation

One of the main ways of creating a feeling of safety is to tell people at the beginning of every meeting what the plan is for the meeting. Tell them when it is going to end, who is going to contribute what, and perhaps even what your expectations for the meeting are. Also, segment by segment, particularly when you want a lot of participation, explain what is going to happen. Say to the cell, for example, 'We are going to discuss this and this, and then we are going to pray aloud and give thanks to God for what we have had a look at.' Or: 'We are going to look at the subject of the father heart of God tonight. Two or three people are going to share how God has become a father to them, and if anyone is struggling in this area, we are going to give the opportunity for them to receive prayer.'

The mission organization Youth With A Mission (YWAM) discovered the strength of this in a bizarre way. For many years, certain groups of YWAMers went on three-month field trips to the Holy Land, exploring some of the lands and places where the New Testament was lived out and written. Meals could be very erratic during these trips, and many people would pile on a huge amount of weight. One girl on the team made the following observation: 'The reason people are putting on weight is they never know if this is the last meal they're going to get for a while, or what might be in the next meal. So they eat like they'll never get another meal.' She encouraged the team leaders to say at the beginning of each day what would be served at each meal, which meal would have seconds, and what the approximate serving time would be. This simple explanation brought safety. People didn't pig out any more because they knew that they would still be able to eat as much as they wanted at the next meal.

For church leaders, this principle of explaining things beforehand might be good to bear in mind not only for one's cell, but also for the Sunday service. Many well-intentioned church meetings can turn out to be very scary experiences for strangers who are visiting. The person at the front of the meeting doesn't say who they are or why they are leading the meeting, and the visitor is given no idea as to the length or shape of the service. Then bizarre things happen: people dance, speak in strange languages, fall over as if dead, and so on. All of which is often greeted with great enthusiasm by those in the know, but the poor visitor is not only bemused, he or she has definitely made a mental note never to darken the doors of this establishment again. All that is needed is just a simple bit of explanation, with the leaders introducing themselves, and saying what is going to happen during the meeting. Then, if something out of the ordinary occurs, the leader will give a very quick explanation. That way, there will immediately be an environment of safety. The individual will know exactly what is happening and hopefully choose to come again.

7. Body language

The cell leader can use their body language to facilitate the cell meeting. This is easiest to control when the cell leader is leading every segment, as it will take a while for other people to pick this skill up. Perhaps it is most important in the word segment.

In the word section, having meditated on a passage of Scripture, people are asked to share what it means to them. The cell leader may find it useful to turn their body to somebody and look them in the eyes; in that sense they are given a clear signal that they can share. This is their opportunity. It is important to develop this skill, as in your cell you may have a few well-known characters such as: Mr or Ms Dominate, Mr or Ms Introvert, and Mr or Ms I Like to Hear My Voice All the Time. These individuals need to be quietly but firmly dealt with. By looking at a quiet person, and with the cell leader's body clearly signalling 'This is your time', it helps them to realize that now they are able to speak. Remember to affirm them at the end of their contribution.

If, in any one segment, Mr I Like to Hear My Voice All the Time has already spoken, turn your body and eyes away from him. Clearly look at other members of the cell and ask if anyone else would like to make a contribution. In a sense, the cell leader is acting a bit like a policeman at a busy cross-section who is stopping one bit of traffic and waving on another bit. If the dominant personality continues to dominate, it might be good to meet with them outside the cell and talk to them about cell values, particularly every member in ministry. Ask them how they could contribute to the cell in making this value a reality. Hopefully, they will come to the conclusion themselves that they should let others contribute as well, and not to dominate all the time. If they don't come to this conclusion themselves, you may have to point it out to them gently.

8. The power of repetition

All forms of repetition are helpful. If in the worship time there are corporate meditations and thoughts shared, write them down. Then repeat them. The use of pen and paper is very important for the cell leader. Whenever these are used, it communicates that what people are contributing is of value. One note of warning, though: always slope the piece of paper towards the cell members. This is so they can see what is being written. If the piece of paper is tilted towards the cell leader and they can only see the back of it, they might assume notes are being taken about a negative aspect of their contribution.

9. Positive listening

When someone speaks in a cell, encourage the person leading the segment to give the cell member their full attention: with positive eye contact, focus of their body and so on.

Positive listening also means learning how to ask questions. Part of the skill of keeping an edification process going involves asking good, open questions, in which the answer cannot simply be 'yes' or 'no'. For example, if you ask a cell member, 'Has this scripture helped you?' they can simply reply with a 'yes' or a 'no' and you have learned nothing. But if you ask them, 'What in this particular verse or scripture has helped you?' they have to answer in more detail. Questions that begin with 'what', 'when', 'how' and 'why' are normally very difficult to say 'yes' or 'no' to.

10. Flow/preparation

As in all meetings, flow is very important. In other words, the meeting has to have some pace to it, some movement. Again, this gets more difficult to control when the cell leader delegates.

The person delegated to needs to know clearly what is expected of them in their segment, particularly in the area of time: 'Please take 15 minutes to do this,' or: 'There are 20 minutes before you should wrap up your section.' If something takes 40 minutes and it could have been done in 20, people will get bored and the meeting will lose dynamic. We have all been to Sunday meetings that have dragged on for more than two hours, when more or less exactly the same content could have been delivered in one-and-a-half hours if people had been a little more disciplined.

An important aspect of flow is the preparation put into the meeting. It would be helpful if the cell leader and assistant leader met, say, at least once a month, preferably twice a month, to look at the meetings with regard to who is going to do what and what is the expectation for each meeting. The rule of thumb is that if we aim at nothing, that will probably be the result. It is important that we have some kind of expectation that we can pray about.

At least one cell meeting per month, and perhaps two, should end with a time of ministry around a particular theme. The cell leader needs to be aiming towards that. Obviously, if the cell has its word section based on what is taught on Sundays, the cell leaders need some prior indication from their leadership on what is going to be taught.

One of the rules of thumb I have used in nearly every message I've preached in the last 20 years is to ask myself, 'What is the "take away"? What do I want people to leave with?' Sometimes this can be a principle for the future, an idea or a value. Sometimes it is a decision or response that you want people to make in the meeting, so that they can be prayed for. The cell leaders may want to have a clear idea as to what it is they want people to take away over a series of meetings, as well as from a particular meeting.

Cell ministry and community building

Many times in previous chapters, we have referred to the significance of ministry in the cell. Perhaps the most noticeable form of this is when someone expresses a need. This could happen in the welcome section or in the worship, but it is more likely to happen as part of the word segment, where the cell is encouraged to reach out and pray for individuals. This ministry can take any form, but the cell leader needs to remind people that the gifts of the Spirit, as valuable as they are (and they do need to be strongly encouraged), are not more important than a scripture that someone might read, or even a little bit of advice that someone has. The whole point of ministry is not just that the person who is being ministered to is helped, but also that the cell members feel that their contribution in that ministry time, however big or small, is significant. That will begin to encourage each individual that giving is as good as receiving. As we give our life away, in fact we really find it.

In the ministry time, it is probably best for the cell leader to encourage the person being prayed for to sit in the middle, or to have one or two people quietly sit with them. The cell leader should also state clearly what it is he or she expects to happen: 'Let us pray for John. Maybe you have a scripture, a piece of advice, a word of knowledge, a prophecy, or just an encouraging prayer for him.' The cell leader should not contribute first, instead praying towards the end so that it is the cell members who are initiating the ministry time. While this is going on, the cell leader can be asking him or herself a question: 'What can we do practically as a cell to help this cell member?' For example, in one cell I heard about, a very young, newly married couple were present. It was obvious that the young wife was quite upset. During the word segment she asked for ministry, and basically broke down and cried, and shared how she and her husband were very hard up financially. For some reason or other all their money, several hundred pounds in fact, had been in her purse, which the husband had left on a bus and lost. Not only did the cell leader encourage prayer for both of them, he asked the cell to consider ways they could give to that couple financially. During the following week, financial contributions were made from the cell and they almost equalled the amount that was lost. It may not always be possible to tie the ministry into practical demonstrations like this, but cell leaders need to keep reminding themselves that a cell is not a meeting but a community of people. So if there is any way we can practically reinforce the ministry, we need to do this.

In the diagram 'The Stages of Building Christian Community' we see in detail the process that the cell is going to go through. The diagram outlines the goal of the cell at any particular point in time, with problems to be faced, and strategies and activities that would be helpful in dealing with these problems.

One of the areas to be dealt with here is conflict. Cells normally get off to a positive start, but after about three months people begin to make complaints like, 'I am bored with the four "W"s', or, 'I don't like Jane in my group', 'My expectations are not being met', and so on. This may be the crisis point in the cell, and it is here that the cell leader needs the most support from the cell co-ordinator. Let us briefly run through how to deal with this. First, we want the group to face the conflict, and to own it as their problem to face together. It is not the problem of the senior leadership, who imposed the cell structure on the church, nor the cell leader. It is an expected part of the life of the group

The Stages of Building Christian Community

Ephesians 4:16: 'From him the whole body, joined and held together by every supporting ligament, grows and builds itself up in love, as each part does its work.'

STAGE	1 Acquaintance	2 Conflict	3 Community	4 Outreach	5 Multiplication
Other names	Honeymoon Birth and infancy	Conflict Childhood Storming Transition	Community Teenage Norming Community	Ministry Maturing Performing Outreach	Closure Old age and demise Reforming Multiplication
Goal	Getting acquainted	Honesty and worship	Edification	Outreach and ministry	Smooth division
Focus	Group Members focus on the idea of the group	Self Members focus on what the group can do for them	Christ Members lay personal needs down and focus on Christ	The lost Christ turns the attention of the group outwards in ministry	Growth The group experiences cell multiplication
Problems	Insufficient time given to acquaintance-making and helping everyone	Leader does not bring focus onto Christ in worship and his desire to be	No real problems at this stage. Avoid stagnation	Potential to stagnate once community formed, if leader does not	Reluctance to reconfigure and leave old relationships

	to feel comfortable	head over his body	set goals and focus group	Facilitate use of gifts	Plan and communicate well ahead
Strategy	State purpose and goals of group	Face conflict positively	Interest groups	Accountability relationships	Celebrate growth
	Longer ice-breakers	Create ownership	Relational evangelism	Social outreach events	Choose new items
	Social events	Covenants	Prayer walks	Develop intern	Part!
	Discuss need for trust	Ground	Hand over to intern		
Ephesians 4:16	Supporting ligaments	Joined and held together	Grows and builds itself	From him	As each part . . . work[s]
	Pseudo-community	Reality	Fruit of community	True community *love*	*Works*

as everyone gets to know each other. If this is viewed as an opportunity for the Holy Spirit to do a defining work leading to more maturity, then this conflict can be used for good. The goal is that we want to create honesty about the problem and focus the cell around Christ as a solution. In a sense, the cell members have to recognize that the way forward lies in the more mature ones laying their lives down for the other cell members. This is the challenge of self, an opportunity to deal with self for the sake of others and the future of the group. It is obvious that a cell of eight selfish people will not last. Hopefully, the more mature people will begin to lay down their lives and others will be encouraged to follow suit.

Soon after the cell is formed the cell leader may want to begin to lay down some ground rules, and give some suggested guidelines for the cell to own. The cell leader might lead a word segment based on Psalm 46, drawing out principles on how to deal with trouble. One instance would be: 'What are we going to do if any one of us becomes too dominant? Can we agree together that the dominant person would be lovingly approached and encouraged to be less dominant for the sake of the others? And on the same basis, we should keep on lovingly encouraging the quiet members.'

It is important that these two ground rules are worked out in the 'getting to know you' stage of the cell, because dealing with noisy members of a cell and handling positive criticism are two very common problems.

Conclusion

In closing this chapter on the skills needed to be a cell leader, let us go back to our values as seen in the diagram entitled 'Values

Values of Cell Outworked

Values of cell	Us	Cell
1. Jesus at the centre	My relationship with Jesus and the reality of that is my leadership.	a. Faith that he is there. b. Cell member can encounter Jesus and be changed.
2. Every member in ministry	Facilitator leader.	a. Welcome is key. b. Spectator to participator. c. Atmosphere of contribution.
3. Personal growth	How will I develop my relationship with Jesus and experience the dynamic of working with the Holy Spirit?	a. Problem to answer. b. Passive to mobilized. c. Accountability.
4. Multiplication	Growing passion for the lost one to three unchurched friends.	a. As the cell develops this must become more and more central. b. Work through evangelism cycle.
5. Community	a. Hospitality. b. To facilitate the quality of relationship and care inside and outside the meeting.	a. Small number in the cell model. b. Community does not just happen. c. Prayer, care, share. d. Goal: cell members to become community facilitators.
6. Sacrificial love	a. In my world, time, friends, etc. b. My shepherd heart for the group. c. Prayer	a. Underlying value for the cell, which is encouraged at all times.
7. Honesty	My openness creates the environment for people's real problems to surface and be dealt with.	a. Welcome. b. Edification. c. Process that develops.

of Cell Outworked'. Here we see the different values that we are embracing in cell church, how they relate to the cell leader (in the middle column), then what they look like in the cell itself. So the cell leader embraces the values personally, allowing his or her life to be changed, and then by the grace of God sees their cell impacted. All of these values are important, especially how they impact your cell and you as a cell leader. But one value that is especially important at the beginning of a cell is every member in ministry.

One of the early goals of the cell is to arrive at the community stage, and that happens when cell members go from being passive spectators to being mobilized. Maybe they have problems in their lives, some very real and deep problems that they need to be honest about and work on. But this does not stop them from contributing, caring for other cell members, seeing God use them, and being actively involved in the cell community and cell meetings.

Finally, it might be useful to look at another way of thinking about our cells. The following is drawn from what Bill Beckham has written about the five essential cell systems. In a sense, it emphasizes many of the things we have said in this chapter and themes that are picked up in other chapters as well.

In cell church there are some essential systems which inter-relate, which means we cannot ignore one and expect the whole to function well. Bill Beckham, author of the foundational book on cell church, *The Second Reformation*, explains how these systems connect. He uses the image of fingers on a hand, each one with its own distinct function, to represent the cell system.

Thumb

The thumb represents the cell community. In physical terms, the thumb is important to the hand because all the other fingers relate to it. This is one thing that sets human beings apart from animals – man's hand is different because of the thumb. The theological understanding that I have reached in relation to this is Jesus' teaching in John 13–17, and in John's first epistle, regarding Abiding. Abiding in Christ and Christ abiding in us – not just us as individuals but as a community. I believe that in community we are trying to experience what it means for Christ to abide in us and us to abide in Him. This includes nurturing and fellowship, among many other things. The concept of abiding is, I believe, the underlying principle for community. The thumb is community and, as with the thumb and the other fingers, everything else operates out from this.

Little finger

I use the little finger to represent equipping. It reminds me of those who are newly re-born – the babies in Christ. One of the elements of cell church is that we should be able to look after new believers. One of the great tragedies of the one-wing traditional church has been our inability to look after the babies. The cell church, however, has an intentional strategy for caring for the babies – giving birth to them, taking them home from the hospital, and helping them to grow. The one-wing church, of which I have been a part, has not had a way to do that, yet even the pagan world knows how you are supposed to look after babies. You take care of them in families – you don't put them in a warehouse! We had a terrible illustration of that in the stories that came out of certain Eastern European orphanages. Yet within the church, for the past 1,700 years, new believers have so often been warehoused – on Sundays and at other large gatherings. A cell is a family in which new babies in Christ can be nurtured and equipped. If we are not prepared to look after the new babies, how can God bless us? I like the way that Ralph Neighbour's equipping track materials begin and end with a focus on new believers, taking them to the point where they become fathers, and lead others.

Ring finger

Next is the ring finger, which represents accountability. Many
people in the Western world wear a ring on that finger as a symbol
of commitment to one another. It declares that we are going to love
and be there for each other, come alongside, encourage, and
admonish each other. This relates to the teaching Jesus gave on the
Holy Spirit. He said that there would be one like Him, whom He
would send, who would be an advocate – one who comes alongside.
What a beautiful picture for those first disciples. They knew what it
meant for someone to come alongside, because Jesus had done just
that. He had walked with them, become part of their lives, loved,
admonished and taught them. This is how accountability should
work in a cell. However, all over the world Christians have rebelled
against the concept of accountability, because they envisage
someone telling them what to do, who to marry, where to live, and
so on. In England I am told that I need to understand that the
English are independent and don't like the idea of accountability.
The reality is, I have been told that about the people in every
country I have visited all over the world! We are all the same. But as
Christians, accountability is an essential part of who we have
become. We are called to live with God and with each other in relationships of accountability. When I am in an accountability relationship with someone, the Holy Spirit within that believer comes
alongside me, and vice versa. This gives new meaning to the idea of
the Holy Spirit being our advocate – not just as an abstract concept,
but one which is lived out through the flesh and blood of a fellow
believer.

Middle finger

The middle finger represents leadership. I believe this goes back to
the very heart of God as father – our parent and leader. It is God's
heart to be a father and to raise up other parents, who will nurture
young children and be accountable for them. It is within the cell that

leaders should be identified, grow and become fathers. Using the analogy of 1 John 1:12–14, it is in the cell that we begin as children, grow into young men, and become fathers. A cell church strategy is one of leadership, which is what Jesus used. It is God's heart to raise up leaders who can help to care for His children.

Index finger

Finally we have the index finger, whose significance is self-explanatory. It is the pointer – we use it to indicate and to direct – and it represents evangelism. This goes back to the heart of God expressed in John 3, 'God so loved the world that he gave his one and only Son'. It goes back to the fact that Jesus came to seek and to save the lost. God's heart is to reach out and touch those who are hurting, lost, and needy. The parable of the Lost Sheep tells of the shepherd who goes out to find the one sheep that is missing when the ninety-nine are safe. Any group that seeks to represent the heart of God must in the end go out to try to touch the hurts and needs in the world, and to reach the lost.

(Taken from *UK Cell*, with permission.)

Summary

- The role of the cell leader is key in a cell church.
- Cell leaders need to be people who love Jesus and can facilitate others to use their gifts and make their contribution. They need to be people who are seeking to live out the values of cell church. The structure of the cell makes the task of cell leading achievable by many more believers. Cell leaders are supported by cell co-ordinators or coaches.
- Some of the tasks of the cell leader are:
  - To lead through facilitating the involvement and ministry of each cell member.

- To initially organize the practicalities of coming together.
- To lead the cell meeting on a weekly basis.
- To facilitate community in the cell group.
- To facilitate the pastoral welfare of each cell member.
- To pray for the cell.

7

Evangelism in the Cell Cycle

In looking at evangelism in the context of the cell, we need to remind ourselves of the values of the paradigm change that we have already suggested. Cell-based evangelism is about every cell member getting out of their Christian ghetto and forming quality relationships with the unchurched. Over a period of time, the Holy Spirit will begin to work through these relationships, and it is to be hoped that at some point in the process, the unchurched person will give his or her life to the Lord.

The fourth 'W' of the cell, the witness section, is there to keep evangelism a high priority, and to empower and encourage all cell members in their relationships. Whatever form of evangelism we are involved in, it is always going to be hard work. Therefore, empowerment and accountability are crucial. So what should this fourth 'W' look like in the cell meeting? Existing cell churches have found the fourth 'W' the hardest part to carry out. So in this chapter we want to lay out a few suggested guidelines, which the cell leader can use creatively.

First, as the cell begins to establish itself, there needs to be an

Strategy for Cell Evangelism and Multiplication

Stage 1	Stage 2	Stage 3
Prayer/Research	**Sowing**	**Multiplication**
For a period of 2 to 6 weeks pray for your area. Identify spiritual strongholds and pray against them.	Each cell member to develop three real friendships with the unchurched in the local area.	1. Pray for individuals in list of 30.
For 1 to 3 weeks discuss what evangelism is. Does everyone understand relational evangelism?	a. Put personal strategy in action.	2. Arrange strategy for reaping.
For 1 to 3 weeks design a personal strategy to make friends with the unchurched and share the strategy around the cell.	b. Start to pray for people by name.	3. Invite friends to Alpha or special events and meetings with gospel content and opportunity to respond.
	c. Outside of cell meetings hold parties and invite cell members and unchurched friends – cell is now building community with churched and unchurched.	
	d. Hold each other accountable to personal strategy. Keep on praying.	
Goal 1	**Goal 2**	**Goal 3**
a. Cell members have a change in their value system re: evangelism.	a. Establish a network of 30 individuals.	For the cell to multiply or at least five people in the network to come to faith.
b. Each cell member designs their own strategy for developing friendship with the unchurched.	b. Prayer re: market-place involvement.	

understanding that at some point multiplication is going to take place. The cell might set a period of time – say, between fifteen months and two years – in which it hopes to have won enough people to Christ for the cell to multiply. It is helpful to look at this process in three stages, which can be seen in the diagram 'Strategy for Cell Evangelism and Multiplication'.

Stage 1 – Understanding evangelism

The first stage, which could take up to three months, is about each cell member having a change of values by understanding what evangelism is and isn't. Having gone through that process, each cell member can then form a strategy to make friends. This particularly applies in the first test cells and real-time cells in the transitioning phase. When cells are well established and they multiply, new cell members should attain these values by going to the equipping weekend on evangelism.

Let us see how this could work in a twelve-week period. For the first five weeks of the cell, it might be good just to pray for the area that you are living in. Ask the cell members what they think are some of the spiritual strongholds in the area. Having identified four or five of these, cry out to God for your area on a week-by-week basis. Then spend the next two or three weeks going round the cell, asking people what they think evangelism is. The goal of these two or three weeks is that in the end each cell member will see that evangelism is about friendship. In the following two to three weeks, break the cell down into pairs or triplets and encourage each member to think through how they are going to make friends in the locality. They should also design a personal strategy for how they are going to do this. As we have said in an earlier chapter on evangelism, we are looking for friendship. This does not mean somebody you wave to every now and again and you think is called Harry or Henry – it should be a genuine relationship.

As cell members do this, the cell leader might want to give some encouragement on how to make friends. We cannot just go out on the streets and be 'friendly' with people, as this will confirm many people's worst fears as to what Christians are like. We need to understand that friendships are formed in the context of something else. We should find a common context in which the Christian and the unchurched person are on an equal footing. This becomes the basis for developing the friendship. It is important that we do this remembering the values that we have already mentioned. One of them is sacrificial love. We are not building friendships for people's converting potential; we are seeking to build friendships because we genuinely care for the world out there. Jesus commanded us to go out and share the love that he gave us, and if we have a genuine friendship, it is of course natural and right that in the context of that we share our love for Christ. If any one of us found a sure-fire way of becoming a millionaire overnight, and we didn't share it with our friends, we wouldn't be a very good friend. Christians can be likened to hungry beggars who have found bread. If we don't tell other hungry beggars where they can find bread, we're not very good friends.

So, motivated by sacrificial love, we begin to build friendships in common contexts. This could be done by participating in an activity in our street, such as Neighbourhood Watch, by joining parent–teacher associations in local schools, by getting involved in the infrastructure of our local community, and also through our leisure activities. The advantage of the leisure activities option is that, in a sense, we all have energy to do the things we like. So if we can combine leisure with our friendship making, this aspect of evangelism is not a chore for us. It's not sapping our energy, but is something we can positively look forward to. There is also the possibility of building friendships where we work, but we need to remember that in today's culture, people don't always work where they live. So local relationships are very important.

At the end of this first stage of the evangelism cycle in the cell, through these twelve weeks, it is to be hoped that two goals will have been achieved. One, that people will have had a change of understanding about what evangelism is and isn't. And two, that each cell member has a strategy that they are going to put into action to make real friendships.

Stage 2 – 'God is good, and we're OK'

Stage 2 of the strategy is what I call the 'God is good, and we're OK' stage. This has two aspects to it. One is that we want the unchurched people's picture of God to be changed – that they see that God is good and Christians are OK. And the second is that slowly but surely some of the content of the gospel is introduced to them. This will probably be the longest part of the evangelism cycle and could last for as long as eight or nine months, or perhaps longer still.

The goal of this second stage is that the cell builds up a corporate network of relationships with unchurched people. If the cell begins with ten members, that will equal about thirty relationships. In other words, we are looking for a ratio of three unchurched friends per cell member. Remember, we are talking about real friendships, people we are spending quality amounts of time with on a monthly basis. As a cell, we should have about thirty people that we are spending time with and regularly praying for over the period of a year. Bear in mind that some of these people will take many years to open up to wanting to know more about Christianity. On the other hand, there are others who will be interested fairly quickly, and can be brought into the third and final stage of the cell evangelism cycle.

However, in developing these relationships over the second stage, there are a number of things which need to take place. In stage 1, the cell's prayer is general and is mainly for the area it is based in. In stage 2, the cell should now begin to pray for the genuine relationships that the cell members have. The prayers will become much more specific around those individuals.

The first three or four months in the life of the cell are about building community among cell members. But now, slowly but surely, unchurched people are being joined into the wider community of the cell through friendships. By the time of the third stage of the cell cycle our unchurched friends should actually know other cell members and not just the initial contact. That way, they form part of an extended community. One way to build this extended community would be to have a party, rather than a cell social event to invite people to. People are happier in the early stages to come to something they understand, like a party. Maybe all cell members could have a party on their birthdays, and invite their unchurched friends and a few cell members. If they can think of a few other reasons to have a party, all the better. Instead of having a cell barbecue, one of the cell members should throw a party that just happens to be a barbecue.

There are a number of significant advantages to this. One is that if someone is invited to a party, there is an implicit obligation on them to return the invitation. This is extremely beneficial, because at our friends' parties, we get to see them within their normal context and can get to know their unchurched friends. However, if we invite people to a cell event, there is no pressure on them to return the invitation, as they don't have an equivalent event that they can invite us to. After a good number of months, the cell could probably run social events that it does invite people to in a slightly more formal way, and the contents might have something more of the gospel in them. During this time, be aware of any needs that your friends might have. If you can't help them, maybe another cell member can.

In the actual cell meetings in the stage 2 period the cell members should regularly be holding each other accountable, sharing how their friendships are developing, and praying for them.

The 'party party' strategy that I have outlined above will obviously work particularly well in a middle-class culture. This may need reinterpreting and rethinking for different ethnic groups or social groups that we might want to be reaching.

Stage 3 – Multiplication

In the latter part of the cell cycle (this could be a year and a half into the cell), having built up a network of relationships, having prayed for individuals on a regular and individual basis, we need to think about multiplying the cell and reaping these individuals into the kingdom. It is, of course, possible that some people may already have given their lives to Christ during the course of the previous year, as they may have come into contact with something of the kingdom before meeting a cell member. But what we need to establish here is a regular harvesting/reaping cycle.

First, let's talk about the Alpha course. There is absolutely no doubt that Alpha as a strategy is a gift of God for the moment.

It is a way that people can be reaped into the kingdom that fits into the principles of the new paradigm. It is relational; it is a process; it has content. Many of the cell churches set up during the last few years have grown through the use of Alpha. Alpha has followed two basic models. First, there is the major, church-run Alpha, which often fits in with the October national advertising campaign around Britain. This is where the Alpha course is led and inspired by the main leaders of the church. It is probably put on in a big facility. If the church has cells, then each cell might be challenged to take on a table at the course. At some point in, say, July, that cell might have an Alpha cheese and wine evening, where the idea of Alpha is introduced to non-Christians and they are then invited to the October course.

It is to be hoped that each cell might have five unchurched friends and perhaps three cell members who are on that course. If our previous strategy has worked (building some kind of community that has included these non-Christians), the chances are that they will know all the cell members on their particular table, and even some of the unchurched people. If they give their lives to Christ, because of their relationships, the cell is the most obvious thing for them to join. The beauty of this particular way of doing Alpha is that everybody in the church knows it is going to happen in October and will have something to aim and pray for. As we all know, network evangelism is hard work – it takes energy. It is good to have clear, fixed goals that people can be held accountable to, pray for and think about.

The second basic model of Alpha is much smaller. Instead of anywhere between forty and several hundred people attending, as in the first example, it may just be five to ten. In this second model, a cell might decide that since some of the people in their network are showing tremendous interest in Jesus, now is the time for them. Rather than wait for the October Alpha, the cell can run a cell-based Alpha course at any time. They might link up with another cell, and those two cells could run the course. In real terms, this second model will impact the cell more than the first. This is because in order to run an Alpha course, the cell might not be able to meet quite as regularly, or it might have to sacrifice one or two members who ordinarily come as they need to put their energy into that Alpha meeting.

Another important harvesting and reaping strategy would be what we call making the most of Christmas. This may not be so much about seeing people make decisions, but it does lend itself very well to putting the content of what it means to be a Christian into people's minds. There is absolutely no doubt that at Christmas time people will come along to events in a way they will not do at any other time of the year. Again, this is a way in which the church at large can serve the cells: by putting on a series of events at Christmas that appeal across the age ranges and cultural groupings.

For example, one church that has a regular summer holiday week for unchurched children will do something special at Christmas where many of those children might be involved in a play or show with a Christmas theme that parents are invited to. Because little Johnny and Sally are in it, all the parents will come along, and in a low-key way the content of the gospel is put across.

Another group in Harpenden, called Stable Rock, have come up with a creative idea for adults. They act out and narrate the Christmas story, but with a difference: they use pop music from the 1960s, 1970s and 1980s. So King Herod enters, singing, 'Do you wanna be in my gang, my gang, my gang?' In a fun way, this is a powerful presentation of the Christmas story. People are invited to a nice auditorium where tables are set up with cheese and wine, and it is a real night out.

It might be good to do a classic carol service of nine lessons and carols. This would be a great opportunity for a church to explore its creativity, and to encourage and challenge members to come up with ideas that will be a blessing to the whole. Obviously the cell will pray about these things and invite their friends, and the events will be put on using the resources of the wider church.

If the 'make the most of Christmas' strategy has been success-ful, a few meetings of a guest-type nature can be put on in February and March, perhaps based on the Willow Creek model: meetings where people hear a low-key presentation of the gospel, and are invited to join an Alpha course or whatever is appropriate.

As we become more outward looking as a church, it might be that we not only have non-Christians dropping into our cells to observe them, but more coming along to our Sunday meetings. A word of warning, though: as church leaders, I think we get into some very bad habits. Once we've encouraged this outward focus and non-Christians begin to turn up at our meetings, perhaps we ought to take heed of a few guidelines. Whoever is leading the meeting should get into the habit of creating a safe environment. They should introduce themselves and tell people exactly what is going to happen, explaining the style of their particular church. If the church is formal, explain that. If people swing from chan-deliers in the church, explain it. That way, people won't be fright-ened when something happens, because they already know. If, perchance, something out of the ordinary takes place, be swift to get up and explain what has happened. Being guest-aware in this kind of way creates a safe and positive environment. We can all tell stories of the grim experiences unchurched people have had when the unexplained and downright bizarre has taken place in our meetings. To avoid this, put on guest services using a very clear format, with a little bit of worship and two or three testimonies, but not all super-rejoicing testimonies. We need to remember that most of the people who come as visitors to our church are probably struggling with pain or difficult issues, so we need testimonies that relate to the sort of life they might be facing. 'I am unemployed, or I am sick, but this is how God is sustaining me and helping me through this experience.' There should be a preached message that is short and to the point, followed by a non-threatening, non-confrontational invitation to respond.

So our evangelism cycle should be supported by the cell and the wider church. Obviously a great deal of the hard work will be done at an individual and cell level, but there is also a role for the wider church and its resources in serving in the area of evangelism.

Everything we have indicated here is true for young people as well. If we have youth cells, we need appropriate harvesting strategies for them. They might be different strategies than the ones we have discussed, more wild, more 'youth culture', but the same basic principles will apply.

Witness/works

In this fourth 'W' we have so far emphasized our praying for the lost, our making of unchurched friends, and how we might see them won to Christ. We also at this point want to emphasize that the 'W' stands for witness/works. Through our value of every member in ministry, we will recognize that people are called to the market-place. They have a salt and light mandate, and we need to encourage them in this.

We have discussed in Chapter 5 how Christians often feel under-resourced and under-cared for, so in this fourth 'W' we want to take the opportunity of inviting people to share what they do at work – what are the ethical and moral issues they face each day. As a cell, we should then gather round them, affirming their calling and praying for them in this ministry.

Both in our cell and in the wider celebration, we should get into some good habits. Every time somebody takes a new job, we should send them out as we would a missionary, praying for them and believing that God is going to use them in their new context. At the cell level, we need continually to look for different ways we can support our cell members who are involved in the market-place.

Outward focused

This overall outward focus we are seeking to create will be one of the hardest things we'll ever attempt. It will take all of the energy and inspiration of our leaders to keep us on track. It is so easy to slip back into non-confrontational, non-relational, isolated Christianity where we long for some kind of 'revival' that requires us to expend as little time and energy as possible.

Ben Wong, a cell church pioneer in Hong Kong, was seeking to change the culture of his church. He asked his musicians to make every fourth or fifth song in their services outward focused in nature, songs about what we have to do on behalf of God. His musicians thought about this and after a few days they came back to him, saying it was impossible. 'There aren't enough songs of an outward nature,' they said, 'so we're going to spend our time singing the same old songs.' Ben Wong wasn't having any of this, so he challenged them to write new ones. It took three to five years of extremely hard work on the part of Ben and his church leaders to turn the environment around from the attitude that if you had non-Christian friends and a network you were somewhat peculiar. Finally, they got to the place where the situation was reversed – that you were peculiar if you didn't have unchurched friends and a network.

Let us be as creative and dynamic as possible in thinking about how we can confront the culture of our church. Through the cell, through the big meetings, through everything we are doing, we need to give church that missionary edge. We are, as the well-known Anglican Robert Warren would say, a missionary congregation. Through our corporate life in cells and celebrations we are genuinely seeking to impact our locality in terms of evangelism, witness and social action. We are seeking through the ministry of our church members to touch the market-place all around us.

We have looked at the theory of evangelism and how it works within the cell church, but what is present-day experience? The lesson that has been observed so far is that changing culture is hard work, and that the simple challenge of asking every cell member to have three unchurched friends may sound simple in theory, but in practice it is hard work. We've also learned that it is easy for the witness section to get lost, and many cell churches, after the initial few months of the cell, change the internal structure to be welcome, worship, witness and word. In our culture we find it difficult to hold each other accountable, so we need to keep empowering our cell leaders to ask loving questions and to push us to pray for our friends and to reach out. However, the good news is that many cell churches that have pushed through and seen their networks grow are, through their partnership with Alpha, seeing tremendous growth. A number of churches have doubled in size and many of those who had seen no breakthrough for many years have now seen one, and people are being won to Christ and discipled. A number of cell churches have even seen new converts come all the way through to become cell leaders. There is no doubt that there is a dynamic partnership between the cell-based network and Alpha as a harvest event – particularly where churches fix their Alpha push in, say, October, and they work towards that. There is a real excitement and things happen.

The other major lesson that is being learned is that even when we do have a network, it is possible for much of the network to be at the bottom end of the Engle scale and quite resistant to the impact of the gospel. Therefore we have to pray harder. A Christian leader who returned recently from Korea commented that he first went to prayer mountain 20 years ago and it was full. He visited in the early part of the year 2000, and to his amazement found that you could not even get a space to pray. This represents a huge amount of consistent praying over a long period of time. No wonder tens of thousands of people have come to Christ there. So in our cells, and in the witness section of the cell meeting, perhaps we need to have five minutes of consistent and constant prayer during each meeting over the year, crying out for the area we live in, no matter how boring this might become. What will we pray about?

Some research carried out by myself indicates that if you ask the question: 'What holds your friends back from actively pursuing their interest in Christ?' people will come up with four consistent themes: (1) materialism and hedonism, (2) apathy, (3) a negative picture of the church, and (4) fear. When we think about it, we can see that these four areas do represent major blockages that might stop people pursuing an interest in Jesus. Therefore we need to pray very hard that the power of these things might be broken in the area in which we live. In a sense, these things have a right to be there, as we are a materialistic society. Three prayers and a crafty hallelujah are not going to make them go away. If you go back to the analogy of sowing, reaping and keeping, a good farmer prepares the soil and keeps on working on the condition of the soil. The better the soil, the better the results. We are evangelizing in what can only be termed as bad soil conditions. Yet, through prayer, we can change it. In summary, we have learned that the principles behind cell-based evangelism are effective, but they are not magic. It will take time to create an outward-focused group of people. It will take time to build up networks and to see the power of God released into our areas through prayer. Nonetheless, if we pursue these things, the fact is that we will see results every year and, because the nature of the ground is changing, the results can get better and better.

Summary

- Create an outward-focused group with the goal of growing in numbers – multiplication of the cell is success.
- Strategy for cell evangelism:
  - Stage 1: Understanding evangelism – motivate cell members to become witnesses.
  - Stage 2: 'God is good and we're OK' – changing the perception of God and the church by building relationships with unbelievers.
  - Stage 3: Multiplication – introducing people to Jesus through the cell and through relevant 'reaping' events.
- Outward-focused cell groups also encourage cell members as they work in the market-place through the week to see themselves as 'salt and light', affecting the environment in which they work.

8

The Cell Co-ordinator and the Life Cycle of a Cell

Bill Beckham has said that at the heart of a cell church are good cells, and if the cells don't work then cell church doesn't work. If we are saying that the cells are the building blocks of the church, one of the priorities of the leaders of the church is to put their energy and time into making sure cells work.

We have already looked at the role of the cell leader and seen that their training and understanding is crucial. In this chapter we want to add another person to the leadership of the cell church. We will call this person the cell co-ordinator, or cell supervisor, or even the coach. This person is not a full-time member of the leadership team, but his or her role is to take responsibility for two to five cells, but three is probably the best number.

The three key areas of their responsibility are as follows:

1. Dynamics of the group – the cell co-ordinator must have a picture in their mind of what a good cell looks like, and also understand how it develops through to multiplication. Their

142

responsibility is to help the cell leader facilitate healthy cell life.

2. Dynamics of coaching and care – the cell co-ordinator must understand the role of the coach and be able to troubleshoot problems in the cell group, as well as support and encourage the cell leader.

3. Dynamics of vision and leadership – the cell co-ordinator has responsibility to help the cell group develop a vision for their cell group and also work with the cell leader to identify and develop potential leaders.

We will look at these three in more detail later in this chapter.

So why exactly do we need someone in this role? It is essential that cell leaders go to leaders' meetings for vision, encouragement, the sharing of problems, brainstorming and so on – and the leader may well think that that is enough. In reality, though, when cell leaders share in a meeting of this nature, they often tell lies – not intentionally, of course. For example, you can have somebody who says, 'My cell is going fantastically, and everybody is enjoying themselves.' What they really mean by this is: 'I am doing all the talking; I'm enjoying the sound of what I'm saying, and I'm sure everyone else does.' In other words, the cell still functions like an old house group and is very leader-centred. In contrast, you could have a cell leader who says, 'My group is a disaster. It's not really working. It's not going anywhere.' Then, when you visit that group, you may say to yourself, 'I don't know what he was talking about. This group is fine. There is no problem here.'

In other words, cell leaders, and especially new ones (and it is to be hoped that there will always be new cell leaders because of multiplication), may not really know the difference between a good cell and a bad cell. Therefore, we need this key individual called the cell co-ordinator, or supervisor, or coach, whose responsibility it is to visit the cells they're looking after perhaps once a month, and also to meet at least once a month with the cell leader on their own. Through this interaction, they should have a clear picture of the strengths, weaknesses and dynamics of the cell and be able to give the advice, coaching and input that are necessary for the cell to grow and eventually multiply. This person is vital in the development of a cell church. The churches that are growing are the ones that have good coaching structures.

In the early days of a cell church, your coach may not be the most ideal, as the best coach is someone who has successfully led a cell for a couple of years. Given the relative newness of the cell movement, that may not be possible. To start with, you will have to use people who perhaps don't have as much experience as you would like, but hopefully this book and other material on cell churches will enable them still to play a crucial role. Let us look at this role in more detail.

The diagram in Chapter 6 (pages 118–19), on the stages of building Christian community, is one of the most helpful documents produced by the cell church movement worldwide. This simple chart needs to be understood by cell leaders and cell co-ordinators. In summary, it tells us what the life cycle of a cell looks like, the varying goals of the cell, what the group will be focusing on during its life cycle, problems the group will face at each stage, and the strategies for success.

Group dynamics

The first area the cell co-ordinator needs to focus on is the dynamics of the group. A key skill of the cell co-ordinator is to be able to sit in on a meeting and know just what stage the cell is at. The supervisor must have a picture in their mind of where they want the cell to go, and they need to be able to discern whether that development is going to happen. They should also be able to see if there is a problem of one sort or another, then work with the cell leader to overcome it.

If the cell co-ordinator does not understand what a good cell looks like and how the life cycle works, they are just going to get caught up in the minutiae and not serve the cell leaders as dynamically as they could. All cells swerve to rot. It is my opinion that everything we're involved in swerves to rot and we need the help of others and of the Holy Spirit to keep us on the straight and narrow. This is definitely true of cells. For all sorts of reasons, good and bad, they go off track, get stuck and then need help.

If a cell is going to go through the five stages of acquaintance, conflict, community, outreach and multiplication, the sort of questions a cell co-ordinator needs to ask him or herself are: What is the mood of the people in the cell meeting? What stage is this cell at? Where are the values of the cell apparent in the cell? What are the strengths of the cell? What are the weaknesses of the cell? What can I do to bring the cell to the next stage?

So as the cell coach sits in the meeting, they need to be diagnosing where the cell is in relation to a healthy plumb-line. Then they should think through with the cell leader what the strategy is for that particular stage, how it can be implemented, and how it will be monitored and evaluated. Obviously this process is a tremendous challenge and it does need maturity. The good news for us is that the skills required for this coaching are the skills that are frequently used in the workplace and can be transferred to support the cells. It is still difficult, though, because describing feelings around a situation that can change from week to week is

difficult, especially when there could be any number of reasons
why a problem occurs in the cell. It could be a difficult cell
member, or maybe the cell leader doesn't have quite enough confidence or experience to steer the meeting back to where it should
be.

Common problems

So what are some of the common problems to watch out for? In
the early stages of a cell, one of the problems may be dominant
cell members, extroverts who never stop talking, and therefore
participation levels die down. Or maybe there are other people
who, for various reasons, feel unable to contribute. The cell
leader could need some practical coaching on how to deal with
this. In Chapter 6, there were some suggestions made regarding
this particular problem, particularly through the use of body
language and eye contact. If these more subtle methods don't
work, a cell leader may need to talk to a cell member in private,
explaining the value of every member in ministry. They should
thank the cell member for their contribution, but point out the
weaknesses of too much contribution and ask that member to
help the cell achieve the goal of every member in ministry, with
everyone participating. This way the cell member isn't just the
problem, but can see themselves as part of the answer.

There are strengths and weaknesses in the four 'W's structure,
and there are definitely two particular problems to watch out for.
One is that some leaders are too legalistic with the structure. In
other words, the temptation is that in their mind they will achieve
all four segments. They have allotted 'x' number of minutes per
segment and no matter what is taking place, whether someone
has become emotional in the welcome segment, or there is an

intensity of Spirit in the worship, and the ministry is very powerful, they move on regardless to achieve their goal of doing all four segments. The structure is only there as a helpful guide – an important guide, but cell leaders must obviously have the freedom to go where the Spirit is going in a particular meeting.

The second major weakness is the opposite. One cell might spend their first 40 or 50 minutes just chattering away. They might always run out of time, and never get to the witness and word sections. They might never challenge each other to make non-Christian friends or to pray for their particular area. In that scenario, they will have lost a major part of what should be happening in their cell. So you see, in one case the cell leader should be commended for hanging loose with the structure; but in the other, the leader needs to be sure that every aspect of the four 'W's is taking place in every meeting.

Another common problem is that the cell becomes just a meeting and there is no real community. For all sorts of reasons, the cell members do not reach out to one another during the week. There is no interaction, other than in the meeting itself. This problem needs to be faced openly and honestly. The cell leader and co-ordinator need to encourage the practical development of Christian community in the cell.

Another problem is when the multiplication strategy is not fully entered into. In British churches especially, this is a crucial problem. The ghettoization of the average British Christian adult, as we have looked at in previous chapters, is a major area of concern. This simple goal of building real community – with each cell member having three non-Christian friends who are loosely built into the life of the cell, who are prayed for on a regular basis, and who at the right time and right place are invited into the reaping strategy of the church, be it Alpha or 'make the most of Christmas' – can be extremely hard work. One of the major roles of the coach is to make sure this strategy is being implemented, and that the cell is praying each week for the major hindrances in their locality that stop people coming to faith. The coach should pray for individuals by name, and spend time encouraging people in their market-place endeavours.

Dynamics of coaching

In just a few short pages, we cannot cover everything that needs to be said about the crucial role of cell co-ordinator, but it is important to lay out one or two of the key aspects of coaching. By the use of this word 'coaching', we can probably conjure up a picture in our minds of a person who stands alongside a group of people, an individual who seeks to maximize people's potential, or someone who is concerned about the whole of the person they are working with: mind, soul and body. They normally understand something of the dynamics of what they are trying to impart and have a proven track record of theoretical and practical success.

A dynamic coach can draw out of a team or an individual levels of skill or levels of play that nobody would have thought possible. In a sense, this is what the cell co-ordinator is attempting to do in their coaching role, particularly as they relate to the cell leader. But it is important at the beginning of any relationship of this nature to lay down some guidelines and expectations.

The first, and perhaps most important, guideline is to seek permission from the cell leader for you to coach them, and then ask how they want it to happen. So if, for example, the coach sees two or three things wrong in a particular meeting, how does the cell leader want the coach to respond to that? Do they want it in the face: 'Tell me everything', or do they prefer, say, five pieces of encouragement for every one piece of advice and correction? We need to remember that different people respond in different ways, and many people, due to their own insecurities and backgrounds, see correction as rejection and therefore become defensive. So the asking of permission is vitally important.

For example Tom, a young Christian leader, had to lead a team of young Christians into a difficult place a long, long way from any support or help. He decided that the best way of working with his team was to ask that if he saw any character weaknesses in their lives, could he have permission to come and share it with them? One person on that team was Peter. Peter was a wonderful young man, but he had two weaknesses. First, he was excessively greedy, and when he sat down for a meal he made sure he had more than anyone else, ate his dessert before he was meant to and so on. This soon began to really annoy other team members. His second weakness was that he asked questions incessantly. Not that there is anything wrong with asking 'why' and 'what' every now and then, but there is a time and a place. Tom realized he had a problem when he saw the well-known missionary the team were working with hiding behind a pillar in his own compound.

Tom asked, 'Why are you hiding?'

'Peter's coming,' he hissed. So Tom hid with him.

Tom realized that he needed to deal with this situation, so at the next appropriate moment he asked Peter to come and spend some time with him. When they met, Tom said, 'Do you remember that conversation where I asked permission that if I saw anything in your life I could share it with you?'

'Yes, I remember,' said Peter.

'Does that still hold today?'

'Oh yes,' said Peter.

So Tom delivered his two observations: 'Peter, you are very greedy, and you ask too many questions, not always in an appropriate manner.'

Peter reacted, but then he remembered that he had given Tom permission and he thanked him. As a result of this conversation, the most wonderful thing took place. Over the next few months, Peter, who'd had these habit patterns for many, many years, began to change. The simple dynamic of asking permission enabled Peter to receive something he might ordinarily not have been able to receive, something which many other people had tried to tell him over the years.

So when it comes to the day-to-day running of the cell, permission must be gained for the coach to give his observations to the leader of the cell meeting. That way, expectations are made clear, and hopefully this relationship now has the possibility of working.

A second guideline or expectation is that the cell co-ordinator has responsibility for the pastoral welfare of the cell leader. Once again, a second set of permissions is required: 'Can I have permission to speak into your life personally if I see a blind spot or a character weakness? Would you like me to ask you questions about your home life, whether single or married? Would it be all right if I ask you questions about your thought life, the way you handle your time and money, and so on?' A clear understanding is needed. And the cell co-ordinator may never have to ask any questions like that at all.

Because we believe in honesty, what we really hope will happen with both of the above guidelines is that the cell leaders will be honest and ask for help. But it is true to say that many people, particularly in private areas of their life, may not know that they have a slight problem. Once permission has been given in this pastoral side of the role and expectations are made clear, some wonderful things can take place.

On a personal note, I have found this not only extremely helpful in working with people over many years in one coaching role or another, but in my own personal life I have given permission to a number of people to ask me awkward questions. They can speak to me about the way I may or may not have handled my life, family, work and so on. Obviously we are talking in this chapter about the relationship between a cell leader and a coach, but is this not something we all need in our lives?

Summary

- The cell co-ordinator is vital in the development of the cell church and can help a cell leader to resolve problems at all stages of a Christian community.
- The three areas that the co-ordinator is working on with the cell leader are:
  1. The dynamics of the group itself and how it works.
  2. The dynamics of coaching the cell leader and making sure the group is adequately cared for.
  3. The dynamics of making sure that the cell has vision for itself, but is also in touch with the vision of the overall church and that the cell is an active part of the overall church strategy.

9

Equipping and Accountability

One of the most challenging values in the cell church movement is personal growth – every member growing. The apostle Paul considered it one of his tasks to encourage people to be mature in Christ. And the apostle John, in the epistle 1 John, writes about the different stages of the Christian life in terms of being little children, young men and fathers. There is a spiritual pathway to maturity, yet we all know within our churches and Christian organizations that there are people who haven't grown for years.

The equipping track and the principle of accountability are the means by which a cell church seeks to encourage every believer to take personal responsibility for their spiritual growth. Perhaps it even changes their picture of church. So often we can sit in church and say that it is the responsibility of the leader to make us grow: 'If they preach good sermons, I will spiritually grow. If they don't, I will spiritually stagnate, but it's not my fault. If my church is a wonderfully loving place, if everyone cares for one another and I'm well looked after, I will spiritually grow. But if it has real human beings in it and sometimes I get damaged, I don't have to grow. If life is always good to me, and I never have a problem or difficulty, then I will spiritually grow; if it isn't, it's not my fault.' Although I've exaggerated here, this does seem to be the prevailing attitude. Yet surely the ministry of Jesus, the apostle Paul and other Christian leaders throughout the centuries wasn't about that. They created an environment that said, 'Yes, leadership has some responsibility; yes, your church has some responsibilities; but the bottom line is that you are a follower of Jesus and you need to grow and take personal responsibility for that.'

Ralph Neighbour, one of the architects of the modern cell movement, is not only an evangelist but also an educator. He has encouraged and developed the idea of what he calls an equipping track. He identifies a simple pathway to spiritual maturity, then provides materials that the individual works through themselves. Having done this, the individual then meets with a friend who is an accountable prayer partner – or, in cell language, a sponsor – and that prayer partner or sponsor asks them how they got on with the material. Have they completed the material? What problems did they have? This gives the individual the opportunity to share what difficulties they might have encountered, and what they have learned or not learned.

You might say, 'What's new about this?' Well, there are several interesting dynamics. First of all, there is the dynamic of personal responsibility. The individual is saying, 'I will take responsibility for my own spiritual growth, and I will work through this material so that I can grow.' The second interesting dynamic is that Ralph Neighbour has designed a curriculum of material. It is this curriculum that is important. Whether the material you use that supports the curriculum comes from Ralph Neighbour

or Lawrence Khong isn't all that important. It is the purpose of
the curriculum to bring every individual to a level of maturity so
that they will become part of the answer, not part of the
problem. They can be active within the cell; they can have a
network of unreached friends, and they can lead someone to
Christ. Christian values will affect their marriages, their finances
and relationships, and they will be able to take Christ out into
their market-place, the world they live in. The third dynamic is
that individuals should have an accountable relationship with
somebody who is encouraging them, who is answering their
questions and is praying for them in this process. As you can see,
this is a unique and very distinct set of dynamics.

Lastly, Ralph Neighbour has identified two other very interesting dynamics. One is that the Christians who are going
through this equipping track are actually being discipled by the
material in relationship to a person. Using materials stops some
of the abuses that happened in the old shepherding movement,
where an individual out of their own head and understanding
discipled another individual. This worked well sometimes, providing that the individual had an adequate picture of
Christianity themselves and didn't have some slightly 'off' ideas.
In the old shepherding system, all sorts of weird and wonderful
ideas were communicated from one person to another. In the
worst extremes, the person being discipled would wash the car or
end up doing the garden of the person who was discipling them,
because that was what 'God wanted'. The dynamic of using
material is that there is a plumb-line with which the church
leaders can all be happy. Everybody is learning the same thing,
and there is the security that it doesn't have some weird and
wacky ideas in it. In the process of the discipleship, individuals
are not becoming dependent on another person. Instead, the

material is encouraging them in their personal relationship with God.

The second of these further dynamics is that the role of the other person is not as a discipler *per se*, but more as a person who can pray with you and make sure you're doing all right. This is fantastic news if revival breaks out. In an average church, if 40 or 50 people came to Christ we would struggle to have 40 or 50 people mature enough to disciple them. In the equipping track concept, this isn't a problem. All an individual needs to be discipled is: (a) to be part of a cell; (b) to work their way through the material over a period of one or two years; and (c) for their sponsor or prayer partner to be only a little bit more mature than they are. The sponsor's main role involves being there if the individual needs advice, a little bit of accountability ('Are you going through the material?'), and lots of prayer and encouragement. Using the equipping track process, cell church could bring a lot of people to maturity with very few difficulties at all. We will look at the equipping track materials later in this chapter.

Encounter weekends

A cell church will also use what we want to call encounter weekends. As we all know, and have seen for years in the Christian life, something special happens when you take a group of people away somewhere, or create a special environment for them. People grow during these times, when you expose them to the teaching and ministry of an individual or group of individuals who have a lot of gifting, experience and anointing.

The cell church takes this idea and makes it an intentional part of its strategy in helping people to grow spiritually. So there will be at least four weekends which every new convert or person joining the church needs to go through. The four weekends should cover the following loose curriculum, but can vary a little from church to church. 'Weekend' can mean Friday night to Sunday afternoon at a conference centre, or any part of a weekend, based at home, for example Friday evening and Saturday morning.

Weekend 1: Formation

The first is what is called a formation weekend. There will most likely be two groups of people at this weekend: some might be new converts, and others may have been Christians for a long time but want to join your church. With this in mind, there should be two streams running through the weekend.

In the stream for the new converts, you could go over the basics of what it really means to be a Christian. Is Christ at the centre? Are we living for ourselves, or are we living for Jesus? Have we really surrendered in a process of confession? Since we have so often preached a benefit-based gospel, we often have people who have not really encountered Christ. We need to make sure that people really have met with Christ and are beginning the journey of following him.

For those who are already Christians, we want to explain the dynamic of every member growing. We should challenge them to mature as Christians and to experience basic discipleship. The sad fact is that many people have been Christians for a long time without changing their value systems. They are trying to live out their Christianity, but their problem is that in their heads and hearts they still have a worldly value system. The way they handle their money, the way they treat their wives, their children and other people is still worldly. This will become an increasingly important issue to us, as the values of Christianity are no longer the values of our culture. We have to encourage people to re-educate themselves with Christian values. We should challenge all those who join our church to begin this transformational pathway. This could perhaps be done on the Friday night, in the opening session of your weekend. On the Saturday morning, you could bring the two streams together and introduce the two groups of people to the values of your particular church. What is your distinctive? What is God saying to you that is special to your area? What is your financial policy in terms of tithing? And so on.

Lastly, and very importantly, you introduce people to the idea that your theological picture of church is that church is expressed in both the big and the small. So, in joining your particular church, cell and celebration are an integral part of the mix. To be a member of the church, the individual needs to be a member of a cell.

That is the loose curriculum for the first weekend.

Weekend 2: Evangelism

The second weekend should be all about evangelism, based on the ideas shared in earlier chapters, as well as other books on evangelism, including *Sowing, Reaping, Keeping*. Over a period of time, all new Christians and people who have joined the church should learn a relational process of evangelism, and be challenged to have three or four unchurched quality friendships with unchurched people. The weekend will give them practical steps on how to make friends, and help them to see how this will work through the life of the cell. It will clarify the relationship between cell and courses like Alpha, and will also explain the content of the gospel.

Hopefully by the end of the weekend they will be excited and have confidence in this wonderful Christian message that sets people free from the power of selfishness, and liberates them into God's wonderful kingdom. They will see that whether they are five years old or eight, they can influence people to live for Christ. The weekend will give them the tools they need, so that if necessary they could personally lead somebody to Christ. It will also explain how Alpha and other church-based strategies work, so that they don't have to lead people to Christ personally but encourage them to join a course like Alpha that will do this for them. Every person in our church will be evangelistically equipped and outwardly mobilized.

Another session in the weekend should be about our marketplace destiny, and the salt and light challenge in the gospel.

Weekend 3: Healing and restoration

The third weekend is for healing and restoration. Many new converts will enter our churches severely damaged, some because of the consequences of their own selfish lifestyles and bad decisions, others because they have suffered through the selfishness of other people. As we know, many people who have been Christians for a long time have not always dealt with the 'giants' in their lives. They are still carrying around major hurts and difficulties. As a result they find it hard to join in and be productive members of the cell.

So in this particular weekend, these individuals are exposed to people who understand how and why we are damaged. They can begin to understand why they have a poor picture of themselves, why they are insecure, or whatever their problem might be. Then they can have an opportunity to experience the healing of Christ.

Acts 3:19–20 says, 'Repent, then, and turn to God, so that your sins may be wiped out, that times of refreshing may come from the Lord.' And 1 John 1:9 says, 'If we confess our sins, he is faithful and just and will forgive us our sins and purify us from all unrighteousness.' In both these passages we have a process that leads to healing. We see that there are some things we must do. We need to confess. We need to own up to our hurts and to our sins. We need to be honest about our backgrounds. We perhaps need to face things that we have kept locked up inside ourselves for a very long time.

Jonathan, a well-known Christian leader, ran into some problems in his own family. He had a child who was exhibiting all sorts of difficult behaviour. Jonathan's wife was confronting their boy and seeking to lay down some strong boundaries, so that he could understand that his behaviour was wrong. Jonathan, however, was always very abstract, and instead of being cross with his child's deviant behaviour and confronting him, he found himself wanting to protect him and just letting it go. But other siblings were being badly damaged. The marriage was under stress, and Jonathan seemed unable to realize that actually he had a problem. Eventually Jonathan had to come to that place where he was prepared to be honest. He was encouraged by his cell to see a psychologist. The psychologist, not a Christian, very soon identified in him what he called 'the Harrod's syndrome'. Jonathan had grown up in a family where there was a great deal of violence between his father and mother. As a young child, whenever he had been exposed to the anger and deviant behaviour of his father, he had been taken away to Harrod's and pampered and cosseted and was able to buy whatever toy he wanted. What this produced in the long term was a weakness in Jonathan's personality: he could not face conflict. Whenever he saw any, he just wanted to take the person concerned to Harrod's (metaphorically speaking) and say, 'There, there, it will be all right.'

With help from his cell and the psychologist, Jonathan realized he had a problem. It wasn't right to run away from every confrontation. He had to have enough healing in his life to be able to say to his child, who was behaving in a totally inappropriate way, that there are boundaries. Jonathan and his wife had to come to an agreement that some things were indeed wrong, and together they could have boundaries for how their children should behave. When Jonathan faced these difficulties and began to respond to his child in a loving, much firmer and at times slightly more confrontational manner, the child was a lot less confused. He came face to face with parents who were actually in agreement, and his difficult behaviour ran into a loving brick wall. Slowly, the child began to respond and change.

The purpose of this story is to illustrate the fact that whether we're a new Christian, or someone like Jonathan who had not only been a Christian for a very long time but had also exercised a lot of leadership in the body of Christ, many of us need healing and transformation. These healing and restoration weekends are not the total answer by any means, but at least they place on the calendar of the church a year-by-year opportunity for us to experience healing. This healing could begin during the weekends, then carry on through the life of the cell and through that individual's personal walk with Christ. It may also encourage the individual to seek counselling, perhaps from a mature person in the church, or, if they have a really significant difficulty, to seek the help of a psychologist.

It is interesting to note that Jonathan's psychologist was not a Christian. We need as Christians to have a wider view of how we are healed. There is no doubt that God can work through the skills of surgeons and doctors and use modern medicine. In the same way, he can use the skills of a psychologist or a psychiatrist. I think that, as evangelical Christians, we have sometimes been suspicious of psychologists, psychiatrists and social workers. It is true that historically some of them were influenced by Freudian and other methods that may be contradictory to some of our Christian presuppositions, but today many psychologists and psychiatrists use approaches that are not inherently anti-Christian.

Honesty and confession are vital in the healing process, and the weekends create an environment for them to take place. But there is no doubt that there is an aspect of Christian wholeness that no psychologist, no psychiatrist, no pill can take care of. Only God can take away the pain of our emotional and sin damage. Psychologists or psychiatrists may be able to point out where the problem is; they can dispense medicine that might alleviate some of the symptoms, but it is only God who brings healing. He is the one who brings times of refreshing and who cleanses us.

I am sure we can all look back into our times of Christian ministry and remember instances of people made whole who had once been damaged beyond all recognition. There is no doubt that some Christian leaders have a calling and an anointing to help bring about this wholeness and healing. In the cell movement, we believe in every member in ministry, but that does not mean that everybody's ministry is the same. Neither does it mean that we all carry the same level of anointing. Certain individuals whom God has called have an anointing that relates to their particular calling. These weekends enable us to expose our church members to such individuals. Can you imagine what the church across the nation would be like if many of our damaged and broken-winged Christians who sit in our churches were restored to wholeness and able to exercise their God-given ministry, and therefore walk in their destiny?

George Verwer, the well-known director of Operation Mobilization, saw a picture many years ago of the true state of the body of Christ. Instead of it being a spiritual army going out to war, the church was more like the walking wounded. Most members of the army were in bandages, walking on crutches, or being carried by others. We want this changed so that, by the grace of God, we can see in our churches more of God's wholeness in the lives of our members.

Going back to Jonathan, having understood new things about himself through his experience with the psychologist, he not only began a process of dealing with these things inside himself, he also sought prayer and asked for healing so that he could feel and act differently. Through the help of the psychologist, and also through the prayer and resourcing of his cell, Jonathan began parenting in a different fashion. This is Christian healing. This is what we want to see. (Please refer to the Resource list at the back of this book for further details on books about healing and healing weekends.)

Weekend 4: Open

The fourth encounter weekend could be open, and different churches may want to do different things. Some cell churches focus on the sponsor's weekend, which is training to help people disciple others using the equipping track materials. Some cell churches have taken it as an opportunity to introduce people to the Bible, with a whole weekend devoted to the Bible. They may do an in-depth look at the Bible as a whole, from beginning to end. They could have an interactive weekend where people, through simple memory games, learn something of the flow between the Old and the New Testaments – which prophets were associated with which kings, and so on.

One of the criticisms that is sometimes aimed at the cell movement is that there aren't regular Bible studies in the cells, which is true. But we do want to introduce people to the Bible and encourage them into a lifelong study and absorption of it. This would make an excellent fourth weekend.

These four weekends should be run every year. As we have already indicated, intentionality is a very important value within cell church. In other words, don't just run these weekends once. By having them on a year-by-year basis, we are making a statement about spiritual growth. Every new convert and every new church member, by experiencing these weekends, realizes that every member growing is both a vision and a possible reality.

Equipping materials

Let us go back to the equipping materials that we alluded to earlier in the chapter. These materials are designed in such a way that an individual is encouraged to take responsibility for their own spiritual growth. The materials provide a pathway for them to spiritual maturity. With each set of materials they have a sponsor who is a cell member; a friend who stands alongside them as they work through the material. The sponsor meets with them maybe once a week or once a fortnight and asks them some questions that relate to the materials. The sponsor in return answers any questions the individual might have, prays for and encourages them.

Since the material is doing the discipling, and the sponsor is

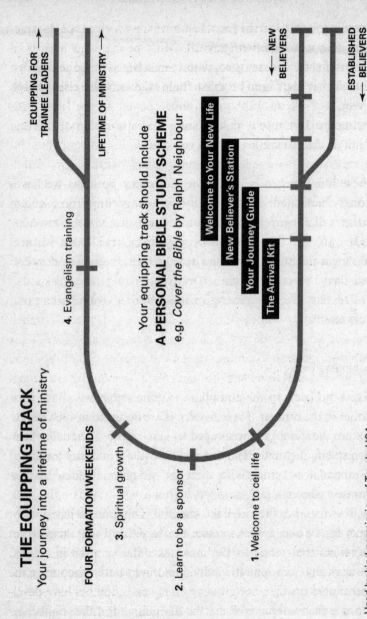

THE EQUIPPING TRACK
Your journey into a lifetime of ministry

FOUR FORMATION WEEKENDS

EQUIPPING FOR TRAINEE LEADERS →

LIFETIME OF MINISTRY →

4. Evangelism training

3. Spiritual growth

2. Learn to be a sponsor

1. Welcome to cell life

Your equipping track should include
A PERSONAL BIBLE STUDY SCHEME
e.g. *Cover the Bible* by Ralph Neighbour

Welcome to Your New Life

New Believer's Station

Your Journey Guide

The Arrival Kit

NEW BELIEVERS

ESTABLISHED BELIEVERS

Used by kind permission of Touch, USA.

more a sort of spiritual encourager, we have a means of discipleship that can cope with revival. Most people who have been Christians for a year or so, who themselves have gone through these materials, would be able to help take someone else through them.

In the diagram you can see some already printed materials that fulfil the spiritual journey I am going to outline to you. I am recommending materials that have been written by Ralph Neighbour, Lawrence Khong and Daphne Kirk, as well as a youth track that has been written by a number of people. But what is really important is the spiritual journey, not these materials. If you as a church have different materials that you feel more confident with and that achieve better results, feel free to use them.

The first piece of material that is required is something that very basically outlines the conversion process. This is to confirm the decision that the new convert will already have made. They can then move on to a more substantial piece of material, which, in the case of Ralph Neighbour, is called *New Believer's Station*. This they can work through, with the encouragement of a sponsor or a friend. *New Believer's Station* contains 30 studies, to be used over six weeks, which give the individual a firm grounding in what they need to know about themselves, about God and about church. So, there are two pieces of material here for new converts.

The materials then need to change slightly. Your cell might not only have new converts joining, but established Christians from other churches who have perhaps moved into your area or joined your church for whatever reason. Since we want to encourage the value of every member growing, many cell churches have developed a practical piece of material, which, in Ralph Neighbour's case, is called *Your Journey Guide*. This is in fact a spiritual questionnaire. The questionnaire could be filled in by the cell leader visiting the new convert or transfer Christian, spending about 45 minutes with them and getting their permission to ask some questions about their background. This will give the cell leader a clearer picture of the individual's spiritual maturity, indicate where there might be some strongholds in their lives, and also show some areas where they might need more discipleship. The questionnaire sends out a loud message that the cell is a place of spiritual development and growth. *Your Journey Guide* not only looks at areas of personal development that are needed, but also seeks to show people's gifts and ministries so that they can be encouraged in the concept of every member in ministry.

We then move on to another piece of literature, called *The Arrival Kit* in Ralph Neighbour's case. This was written primarily for new Christians, but everyone who joins a cell is encouraged to go through it. It is a fairly unique document, inasmuch as it is designed to help people change their value systems. Too much discipleship deals with actions and not enough with the underlying attitudes and values forming our actions. If you have a value system that basically says you are a nobody and have no personal worth, it will have an impact on your entire Christian life until it is exposed and dealt with. If you have absorbed a value system that says men are superior to women in some way or other, this will radically impact the way you treat other women in the cell and how you treat your wife or girlfriend. Of course, this is true the other way round as well. If a woman has a negative image of men, it will similarly impact her relationships with the opposite sex. An important part of discipling is to have our values changed.

One of the things we are all keen on is the concept of new converts and new church members giving financially as a biblical principle. But the fact of the matter is, it doesn't matter how often you ask people to give or how well you preach about it, unless people have embraced the value of generosity, and until they understand that as Christians we are only stewards and not owners of everything we have, they will not give. So *The Arrival Kit* seeks to disciple people by exposing them to a Christian value system. As our nation becomes more pagan and our converts from unchurched backgrounds have fewer Christian values, things like *The Arrival Kit* will become much more necessary.

If we look into church history we will see that the early, New Testament church had its own equipping track. It was a teaching process over a one- to three-year period. Before a person became a full church member, they were exposed to the beliefs, practices and values of a Christian family. In other words, the early church intentionally discipled people in the ways of Christ. Material like *The Arrival Kit* is seeking to do the same. Again, it is not important necessarily to use Ralph Neighbour's *The Arrival Kit*, or something similar, like *Living Your New Life* by Lawrence Khong. It can be any material that deals with these issues.

Having gone through this material, the next step is for individuals to become sponsors or friends to someone else. To help them, there is a piece of material called *The Sponsor's Guidebook*, which gives practical tips on encouraging others.

The last piece of material should be something on evangelism, and one book I can recommend is called *Sowing, Reaping, Keeping* (see Resources in Appendix 4). Reading the book should ensure that the new convert and the transfer Christian both have an understanding of the process of evangelism and are involved in a network of unchurched contacts and that they are seeking over a period of time – through evangelism, through Alpha, through cell – to win people to Christ.

Conclusion

We have outlined the four weekends. We have outlined the material needed to take people to a certain level. After this, it is up to you. Equipping is for the whole of our spiritual lives. In the secular world, there is the phrase 'lifelong learning'.

At the back of this book, I have identified places you can go to for further material. You may have people of an artistic persuasion in your church who want to be equipped to be effective in this area; you may have individuals with a particular ministry in youth work, leading worship, or countless other skills or giftings. We, as a church, may not be able to equip all these people, but having set the ball rolling we can encourage them to attend the many seminars that are held around the nation, and to read the many good books that have been published. In a sense, we are turning our church into a training centre for the Christian life.

It is our hope and our prayer that every one of our church members will be equipped and inspired for everything that God has for them.

Summary

- The equipping track and the principle of accountability are the means by which a cell church seeks to encourage every believer to take personal responsibility for their spiritual growth.
- The equipping track is a simple pathway to spiritual maturity supported by materials that the individual works through themselves, meeting with a 'sponsor' to process the issues that come up. This encourages the individual believer to:
  - Take responsibility for their own spiritual growth.
  - Be active in the cell group.

- Be involved in an accountable relationship with someone who is encouraging them and praying for them.
- The discipleship process in the cell happens through cell life, through working on the equipping track materials and meeting with a 'sponsor' or prayer partner, who can be a cell member who is only a few steps more mature than the person they are sponsoring.
- The second part of the equipping track consists of four encounter weekends:

1. Formation weekend

For new cell members who are either new Christians or transferring from another church.

Purpose:

- To revisit the basics of being a Christian for the new coverts or to establish the value of every member growing and contributing for those who have been a Christian for a while.
- To establish understanding of the values of cell church.
- To communicate the distinctive of each person's particular church.
- To introduce the theology of church as being expressed in both the large and small communities.

2. Evangelism weekend

An equipping in evangelism to include:

- The principles of relational, process evangelism.
- How to make friendships with unbelievers.
- How evangelism through cell life works.
- The place of prayer.
- Our salt and light mandate in the market-place.

3. Healing and restoration weekend

Individuals have the opportunity of experiencing the healing power of Christ, through confession and taking responsibility for their own hurts and sins. The weekend creates an environment for honesty and an opportunity for increased wholeness.

4. The fourth weekend (subject optional)

Suggestions:

● A weekend looking at the Bible in terms of a survey or its structure.
● Look at the idea of sponsoring, where one believer looks after another believer and, through the use of the equipping material, they are involved in a one-to-one relationship.

10

Youth and Inter-generational Cells

For most of this book we have been looking at cells as they relate to the adult church, but church is about young people, teenagers and children as well. In our thinking, we need to consider them as much a part of church as anybody else.

Children

First of all, let us look at how children aged between four and twelve fit into cells. There are three possible models that relate to this age range:

1. Inter-generational cells: children and adults in a cell together. The children play a part in the cell, since it is as much a meeting for them as it is for the adults.
2. Children's cells: children have their own cells led by adults, and they meet in their own time and place.
3. Children's work as normal: the work is based around a Sunday school, a weekly club or an event.

Let us look at these three models in more detail.

1. Inter-generational cells

The inter-generational cell, which is the most radical of these concepts, works on the idea that as these young people are a part of church, they too have the responsibilities of church. Therefore, they need to be both receivers and participants. They can understand the ways of God; they have the capacity for spirituality, and they can be fully involved. It is definitely not just about them receiving, being looked after or being entertained.

A cell that includes a handful of young people is definitely going to operate in a slightly different way. You have the problem of school times and bedtimes. It is not going to be starting at 8pm on a Thursday night, for instance. An inter-generational cell, in all probability, would best meet on a Saturday or a Sunday, where the adults and children get together for a meal at 4 or 5pm and then have their cell.

As we know by now the cell is broken into four component parts, or the four 'W's: welcome, worship, word and witness. It is the experience of many of the inter-generational cells that young people can take part in at least three of the segments, and a few of them would be able to lead some of the segments as well.

In the welcome section, a generic question is asked, which is designed for everybody to respond to. It can be about life in general, or the events of the past week. Obviously more thought would need to be given to the question so that children have an opportunity to give an answer. Not only do they like taking part, but if given the chance to be in charge of this segment, they can think up the question themselves.

The children can take part in the worship section as well, whether musical or non-musical. It could be a time of listening to music, with people saying how the music speaks to them. It could be a few moments looking at an attribute of the character of God, then thanking God for his faithfulness and love. Or people could sing songs. The main thing is that it should be something everyone can feel comfortable with and be able to contribute to.

In some cell churches, when it is time for the word section, the children go out and have their own segment in this part of the meeting, with an adult or two assigned to look after them. However, with some imagination and keeping the time down to 20 to 30 minutes, it would be possible to involve the children in an interactive-based look at Scripture in the main cell meeting. They too can say what they think, and ask for prayer if needed.

When it comes to the witness segment, children also have unchurched friends whom they want to bring to Jesus. They can be involved in praying and planning how to reach people for Christ.

Now, obviously, inter-generational cells are not going to be for everybody. They will need a little bit more work, and they will take more imagination, but think of the benefits! In church after church, young people come into big congregational meetings armed to the teeth with anti-boredom devices: Walkmans, books, catapults, toys – anything that will keep them amused in the hour or two of agony that they know is going to be inflicted on them. At some point in the service, they might be let out into a Sunday school. In some cases these are excellent, and there are Sunday school leaders who are genuinely and imaginatively seeking to help children have faith for themselves and grow in it. In many cases, though, it's amusement-based: 'Let's keep them quiet, entertain them and hope the preacher doesn't talk for too long.' All this says to young people is that adults, for reasons they keep to themselves, submit themselves every Sunday morning to this incredibly boring experience in the name of Christianity and Jesus. No wonder these young people exercise their own free will as teenagers, and flee the church in their thousands.

In contrast to this, the inter-generational cell shows them that they are church, they can take part, their opinion of spirituality is important, and they need to give and receive just like any adult. If you are going to go down this route, the adults and children need to know that this is not a time for the children to run riot and to dominate. As Daphne Kirk, who is a pioneer of inter-generational cells within the UK, says, 'With children, it is the same as with adults, and therefore the parents must be willing to help their children take part, and this might take some corporate effort on behalf of everybody involved.'

Inter-generational cells offer churches a way that some families and leaders can involve their children. However, not every cell in a church will be inter-generational. In a church with ten or twelve cells, just three or four might be inter-generational.

2. Children's cells

A number of churches are experimenting with the concept of children being in their own cells, with a group of children of a similar age under the leadership of an adult or two, meeting for an hour and a half on a weekly basis with seven or eight children in the cell. It is a place of wackiness, fun and activity, but also a place where the young people can see that they are church, they can give and receive, and they have a responsibility to love God, love one another and love the lost. The meeting is about empowering and encouraging them in their responsibilities – it is not just about being entertained.

In some cases, all the young people in the church would meet together for the first part of the evening. For the first 45 minutes or so they might have fun and play games together. Then, for the next 45 minutes, they would go into their particular cells. Even in this setting the four 'W's can work, but obviously they need to be done in a way that is suitable for children.

3. Children's work as normal

Lastly, we could carry on with life as usual, with Sunday school and whatever children's meetings we can put on. This is obviously better than nothing, but remember that cell church has the value of every member in ministry, with everyone meeting with Jesus and being in community together. Perhaps we should face the reality and responsibility that these values apply just as much to children. We want them to grow up with a dynamic, rather than passive, view of church.

Youth cells

Probably one of the greatest challenges facing the modern Western church is how to reach and disciple this generation of young people. There is no doubt that research shows us that we are seeing adult growth through courses like Alpha and many other things that God is doing at this time. However, the same research also shows us that, week in and week out, hundreds of young people are dissatisfied with institutional church as they find it, and are leaving. This indicates what many of us have suspected for a long time: that there is a crisis facing the church as it relates to winning, keeping and discipling young people. We are facing the full impact of postmodernity in the area of youth work.

In a sense, this presents us with a wonderful opportunity for evangelism, because in postmodernity there is no wholesale rejection of the spirituality of God, as might be found in a more secular modernist view. However, discipleship becomes a lot harder, as there is no acceptance of the Judaic/Christian value system, or for that matter any other value system. In the light of this, we need a whole new approach. Youth cells give us the opportunity to develop new ways of evangelizing, mobilizing and discipling to fit this generation.

In youth work, we have often been forced into situations where we are just looking after the young people (almost like babysitters), and the youth have become consumers of our youth programme. Youth work has traditionally been centred around us wanting to tell young people the truth, and to keep them coming along by providing fun programmes. The bulk of the hard work has been done by a few professional or volunteer youth workers, increasingly pressurized by a need to keep young people of the church away from the unhelpful lifestyles of their non-believing peers. Historically, this approach may have been very successful, but perhaps in our changing times, we need to look at things in a new way. First, we need to be relational, with the truth we want to communicate experienced through that relational encounter. Second, we need to have an empowerment and equipping philosophy, that young people have as much responsibility to love God, love one another and love the lost as anyone else who follows Christ. If we don't enable them to do this, we have sold them short. Third, we want to inspire every young Christian to be a co-worker with God, with them taking the responsibility to evangelize and disciple their friends. Lastly, we don't want a programme – we want a dynamic expression of church, which young people can own themselves and which can be adapted to reach the different sub-cultures that young people create for themselves. Youth cells achieve all of this.

Hopefully, a youth cell can be led by a young person – probably someone older than 14. The cells would have the same dynamics and even the same structure as adult cells, but would be done in a way that is culturally appropriate to young people. Over a period of time these young people will be strengthened in their walk with God as they mutually disciple one another and hold each other accountable to relational-based evangelism.

This does not mean the absence of all programmes or meetings. Young people, just like adults, need that dynamic of the bigger meeting. They also need the support of adults. The adult role becomes that of the cell supervisor or coach, who relates closely to the young leaders. They visit the cell meeting regularly and become skilled in staying close enough to the cell group to be able to help and influence, while at the same time releasing and empowering the young people to lead their peers.

Churches considering youth cells need to look at youth manuals that deal with this subject. *Cell It*, published by YWAM, gives a good foundation on how to run or start youth cells. Further resources are listed in the resource section at the back of this book.

In churches that are experimenting with youth cells, there have been many examples of growth, both in rural areas and the city. In one rural area, a youth cell grew from five young people to 15, so where there was one cell, there are now two. In Southampton, over a period of two years, one cell has grown to 19 cells, containing more than 130 people.

Young people are perhaps the only group in our society who have the social characteristics of historical revival groups – young people live where they 'work' (their schools are local) and they are relational. Every Christian young person knows lots of unchurched people, and has many unchurched friends. So young people, through their cells, can be helped to become authentic Christians whose behaviour is motivated out of a biblical value system. They are encouraged to stand against the weaknesses and influences of postmodernity so that they can embrace Christ into every area of their lives. Then they can begin to influence their many friends at school or college. Instead of being influenced by the culture around them, they are able to make an impact for Christ.

Postmodernity encourages dualism, or an episode-by-episode approach to life. So there are many Christian young people who will be Christian at home and church – in that episode of their life – but at school they may adopt another value system and live another way, so that they are not openly or outwardly Christian. Of course this is not true of all young people, and there are many wonderful young Christians who clearly love God at home and at school. At the same time, though, there are many, many more who live in confusion and dualism. Youth cells offer a powerful dynamic for change.

The process of starting youth cells is, in a sense, much the same as with adults. Leave your church's existing youth work as it is, but perhaps draw out four or five young people who show signs of wanting to grow in God. Run a prototype cell with those young people, led by a youth leader who has embraced the visions and values of cell church. In the cell, use the third 'W' time – the word segment – to challenge the young people about their value system. As the young people experience the power of cell life they become potential cell leaders for the future.

What does our current youth work look like? In many churches we have a youth meeting, and in that meeting we have three sorts of young people: non-Christians, those from a Christian background who think they are Christian, and actively

Christian young people. This mix of people presents a great dilemma for our youth leader. If he or she pitches their meeting at the non-Christians, the Christians are not as challenged as they should be. If he pitches it at the active Christians, then the non-Christians and less enthusiastic Christians are bored. This approach to youth work is a one-box approach: everybody together and everyone in that one programme.

Transitioning to cells and a cell-based approach means seeking to take out a group of young people who really want to go on with God. However, many youth leaders rightly feel that if they take this approach, they will fail in their responsibility to the non-Christians and the Christians who are less enthusiastic. One suggestion is that during this time of transition, a regular youth event is held for the non-Christians, the less enthusiastic and the active Christians to attend. This can be fast moving and relevant, providing an opportunity to explore issues that the young people are facing, showing in a low-key way how a relationship with Jesus can make a difference. An invitation can be made at this event for those who want to join a cell. It should be clearly stated that cells are for those who really want to go on with God. Hopefully, those who go into the cell will be empowered and discipled, and then go back to their friends able to be authentic witnesses.

If we look at the diagram, 'Reaching the unreached', we can see networking at the top, with enthusiastic young Christians out there making friends at school and any other context they can. The next level, entitled 'The Box', is a weekly or fortnightly event with little Christian content, where the emphasis is on hanging out, fun and friendship. This is the old youth meeting, and in this meeting you have a collection of non-Christians who are friends with Christians, committed Christian kids and all shades in between. The third level is the cell, which is peer-led and follows the general principles that have been described. This is backed up by a fortnightly or monthly celebration. The final model could look something like: weekly peer-led cells which gather together for a fortnightly or monthly celebration. These celebrations provide an opportunity for youth-style worship, ministry and teaching and create the sense of belonging to a larger group that young people appreciate. Also in the mix needs to be peer cell leaders' meetings and time for cell coaches to meet with the young leaders.

The cell celebration could be done just for your youth cell, or on a town-wide level. In a town where there are a number of young Christians, but no single church has a massive number of young people, they can gather together for monthly celebrations arranged by youth leaders from all the churches involved. All the cells will be in different schools and churches, and can join together for this regular celebration meeting. That way, local churches still feel an ownership of their young people and yet the young people have the benefit of not only being in a cell but also relating to other Christian young people in the town.

Problems

There are and will be many problems as we seek to become effective in reaching a larger number of postmodern youth. There is no doubt that some of these young people will be attracted to the cells, to have a look at what is going on. But there is a real danger that the cell will turn back into a conventional youth meeting, where unchurched kids come along because they like the community feel and because their friends are there. However, they may not necessarily be interested in going through the four 'W's and they also might find the prayer,

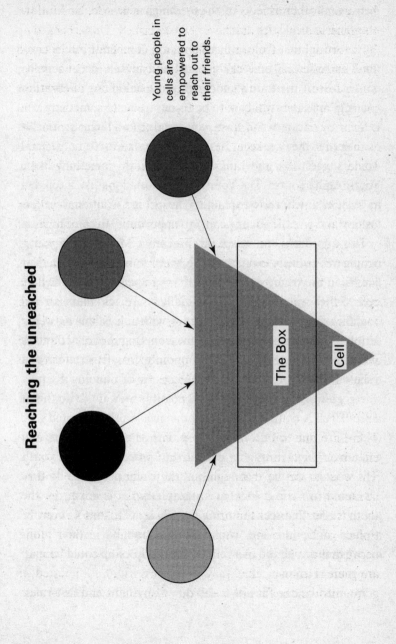

Reaching the unreached

Young people in cells are empowered to reach out to their friends.

The Box

Cell

praise and other aspects of the meetings awkward. So how are we going to deal with this?

It is crucial that the youth cell does not degenerate into a social time, and the real-time cell concept and mutual accountability remains. So, if there are a good number of onlooking unchurched young people, they will have to be encouraged into something else. If there are one or two of them, you could absorb them into the life of the cell if they are keen. But if there are six or seven of them, I would suggest that they are encouraged to do something like a Youth Alpha course. The Youth Alpha could look like a cell, but its basic task will be to explain the gospel in a relational process fashion and give the young people an opportunity to come to faith.

This approach, too, has a few problems. Many of the young people we are likely to attract will have far more problems in their lives than the young people of perhaps 15 years ago. If they are over 15 they will most likely be sexually active, and there is a real possibility that they will be into drugs, with at least one in twenty seriously into drugs. Many will come from dysfunctional families and will therefore carry hurts, disappointments, frustrations and a sense of being rejected. So a real measure of ongoing disciple-ship is going to be needed. If at all possible we want to do this at a peer level. A mature young Christian in a youth cell would seek to form a one-to-one relationship with the new convert and encourage them through a discipleship process. In some youth cells we may not have enough mature young people to do this. Therefore, we could look at a discipleship course run by the youth leader that seeks to bring this young Christian convert to a place of healing and wholeness, and stability in their faith, before they are placed in a cell. Or the discipleship could happen alongside them in a cell.

We must be careful not to lay down any hard and fast rules.

But, at the same time, youth leaders should be given a number of creative options for dealing with the particular problems they are facing. This is while still maintaining cell as the basic building block, and still working in the context of the new paradigm where young people are being empowered and encouraged to be church. This does not mean that the youth leader cannot supplement and serve the wider vision of the youth group by running discipleship courses, celebrations, training programmes or anything else – just as long as they live within the principles of our new approach to youth work.

Summary

- There are three models of working with children in a cell church:
  1. Inter-generational cells: with children and adults together, where children play a part in the cell, since it is as much their meeting as the adults'.
  2. Children's cells: children have cells led by adults and they meet in their own time and place.
  3. Children's work as normal: based around a Sunday school, weekly club or event.
- Young people need to be discipled relationally, in a way that empowers and equips them to take responsibility to love God, love one another and love the lost. They need to be encouraged as co-workers with God, with the responsibility to evangelize and disciple their friends.
- Peer-led cells gather together for a fortnightly or monthly youth celebration. Cell leaders are supported closely by youth leaders who have embraced cell visions and values and who have experienced cell life for themselves.

11

Leadership: Passion, Purpose and Power

One of the most difficult things facing a church that is transitioning to cell is the change that is required within the leadership team. We have in the course of this book looked at a number of paradigm shifts that have to occur, so you will not be surprised to hear that there is another one at this important level. Not only is this a change for leaders, but also for the people who have become accustomed to leader-centred churches. They need to understand this paradigm shift and learn to have different expectations of leadership.

Leaders need to make sure that their leadership style and attitude is appropriate to the growth of the cell church. Also, they have to face up to an unpleasant reality. If we were to ask members of the body of Christ what the factors are that cause disillusionment among Christians, you might get the usual answers: pain, grief and failure. But perhaps the answer you would not expect, and which scores extremely high in many places, is church members' disillusionment with Christian leaders. Even though we don't want to take upon ourselves all the problems of church, we may need to recognize that indeed we have caused pain and disillusionment in church life. Maybe not deliberately, but often through our ignorance and weaknesses.

So what are some of the things we have to face? It is plain to see that much of the professional training we have received – and for those who have come up through the charismatic movement, the training they have received through observation – has been inappropriate. It has often been strongly influenced by historical models that say church is the celebration and buildings, and ministry in real terms is done by the leaders. So we have picked up many bad and unhelpful habits, which we need to review. However, even though we are looking at a new paradigm and a new way to do leadership, we are definitely not saying that cell churches don't need leadership. A cell model needs as much leadership from the key leaders as any church, perhaps even more so. But it is the style and nature of that leadership that needs a radical overhaul.

Let us look at the cell church paradigm shift:

Old paradigm	New paradigm
'Do it' mentality	'Facilitator training' mentality
Entertainment emphasis	Empowerment
Focus is celebration	Focus is the cells
Ministry of the few	Ministry of the many
Directive style of leadership	Envisionary, purposeful style
My vision	Our vision
Maintenance	Growth

'Do it' versus facilitating

A verse in Scripture that is well known to every leader, yet is carried out by very few of us, is written by Paul in Ephesians

4:12. Loosely paraphrased, it says that leaders are here to equip saints for the work. The underlying emphasis of this verse is that we need leaders and they have gifts, but the focus of their gifts is to empower, train and equip others to actually do the work. Now why don't leaders do this? There are all sorts of good reasons. In many ways it is far easier to do it ourselves. It is quicker, and we can probably get the results we want. But the fact is, the moment we fall into that kind of trap, we have limited the impact of the body of Christ, and the church or ministry is only as big as the gifts that the leaders have. Whereas if the focus of our gifts is placed in the lives of others so that they are equipped for the work of ministry – be it in the cell, the market-place, in evangelism, caring, worshipping, praying, prophesying, or whatever – there is in fact very little limit to the impact we can make.

Entertainment versus empowerment

One of the things that have insidiously crept up on us in our consumer society is the fact that we as leaders are under pressure to produce better and better church: to run better meetings; to be more dynamic; to improve our creativity – and on and on the list might go.

Here we are caught in a bit of a dilemma, because in one sense we do need to do and be all those things, yet in another sense, we are under pressure to do those things so that we have a better church, or a better consumer product. If that is the case, and we are trying to attract people into our churches by the dynamic of our programme and the power of our personalities, we are falling into the trap of our modern culture and are never going to produce mature Christians. The problem is, the moment someone else comes along who is more dynamic and more creative, the punters will move on, and we the leaders will only be judged by our latest performance.

Instead, we need to enter into a new paradigm of mutual responsibility and empowerment. We are all here to obey the commands of Christ. We all have gifts and responsibilities, and we want to create an environment that says that church in the big and the small, in the market-place and the local, is about all of us fulfilling our responsibilities to God, to one another and to our lost world. We should be involved in church, not because it is a wonderful experience, not because we have the best speaker in town, or the best musicians, but because it is the right thing to do.

Celebration versus cell

The historical model of leadership tells us that the most important thing in church is what happens in the big things, in the buildings and in the celebration. As we have said already, the house church movement started off putting much dynamic into the small, yet even they ended up with a structure that was not very different from the one before.

One of the major shifts for leaders is to fully commit the power of our leadership to the edges of the church, to the cells and to the individuals. That is not to say that we neglect the big meetings and big opportunities, but we have to recognize the gravitational pull, and by stepping into a new paradigm we are shaping our leadership and the way we operate in the light of this new challenge.

The few to the many

It is much easier to work with just a few enthusiasts. Everybody has done it, and who blames them? It is far easier to train and equip those people who come to us and are fully prepared to work with us, even if sometimes their motives are mixed. As the business world says, if you want to get a job done, find a busy person and give it to them. Inevitably, though, this process means that the ministry is done by the few. The extroverted few. The leadership few. The quirky few. Perhaps we've all fallen into one of those groups somewhere in our own spiritual journey.

Somehow we have to break this cycle. As leaders, we have to develop a style and system that says ministry in our church is done by everybody, and we are talking about the broadest possible definition of ministry. From the company director to the youth worker, from the dustman to the counsellor, from the church leader to a seven-year-old, every single person should feel that they are significant in this business called church. Whether they're 'salting and lighting' in their workplace, helping a prostitute in Mile End, preaching on a street corner or running a children's programme, they all have a part to play. This means major change. We will need new atmospheres and new environments in our churches to facilitate this end goal.

Vision and purpose

There are many pictures of leadership in the Old and New Testaments that have influenced us. The Old Testament had the picture of a priest. The Reformation emphasized the priesthood of all believers, yet somehow we still maintained the old paradigm as far as leadership was concerned. It was still the leadership of the priest. In the New Testament we have the shepherd and the sheep. Even though these are good biblical pictures, we end up with a style of leadership that is basically directive, where the vision of the church is the vision of the leader. By and large, what happens in church is what the leader has agreed will happen. The leader sits at the head of the table, whether it's a PCC meeting or a get-together of the eldership. And that leader and a small group of people set the direction.

Is that what they had in the New Testament? Is that what we want today? Perhaps what we really need is a little bit more Holy Spirit anarchy. We, as leaders, can still give something of the big vision and big purpose. We can set out the broad direction that the church is going in, but underneath that will be all sorts of creativity, spiritual entrepreneurism and dozens of other exciting things happening in the life of our church that will never come through an elders' meeting or a PCC.

That is not to say that good things cannot come through the eldership and PCC, but we want a dynamic that says vision, purpose and programmes should not only come from the leaders but also from anyone else in the system. Some ideas may, due to their size and complexity, be run by leaders of more senior experience, but many initiatives from the cell can be done by the cell.

Maintenance versus growth

The cell church leader is taking an irrevocable step in saying that maintenance is not good enough and stepping out into a riskier venture of seeing growth: growth in the people spiritually; growth in the impact the church makes on the local community; growth in the number of people coming to Christ and overall numerical growth for the church. So in a sense they are asking themselves: Is everything that we are doing as leaders helping to facilitate the possibility of growth? Are we giving freedom for God to do all that he wants to do in and through us?

Nehemiah

So here we have the old and the new paradigm. Perhaps one of the best biblical pictures of a new paradigm at work is in the Old Testament. When we look at Nehemiah, we see a wonderful example of a leader who worked within the principles of the new paradigm. Let us look at just some of the highlights of this man's leadership, as seen in the book of Nehemiah.

First, he was a man who was in touch with the heart of God. Have a look at Nehemiah 1:3–5. He was someone who was moved by the situation of his world, who had a passion for God's reputation and God's business. Second, he was a person who was prepared – as we can see in Nehemiah 2 – to place himself in the purposes of God and be a part of the answer. In verse 11 of this chapter he comes to Jerusalem, and here we see some important aspects of new paradigm leadership: he had a vision and a purpose that came from God, and interestingly it was a vision and purpose that was big enough for all the people he subsequently led to play their part in.

Perhaps your vision and purpose is to bring the kingdom of God to a specific people group, or to the geographical area you're in, and the vision and purpose is big. But to Nehemiah it was important that his visionary purpose was defined and researched. He inspected the walls. He knew what state they were in. Then in chapter 2, verse 17, he describes his broad visionary purpose to the people he meets and he allows them to have ownership.

So often churches do not rise to our vision because it is our vision. We have to allow our vision to become the vision of the people. This may be a difficult process. It might take time. But hopefully we will see a significant response, similar to the people in the latter part of verse 18: 'They replied, "Let us start rebuilding." So they began this good work.' Here we see two very different things, which can save us as leaders a vast amount of tears. First, because the vision had become the people's, they did the work. Second, they looked after one another in the process. So we want the people to own our vision and purpose, then they can strengthen and look after themselves in our God-given purpose of cell and celebration.

There was also the fact that Nehemiah delegated, with different groups of people building different bits of the wall. Here my analogy might break down, but perhaps these different groups of people can represent the cells. The walls were being formed, with everybody involved.

Then opposition came. Whether we are in a new paradigm leadership, as I'm calling it, or any other kind of leadership, we will face opposition. Whether it is by cell or any other means, we are not promised a free passage through life. We will face the full onslaught of our spiritual enemies and the negative circumstances that are part of life.

It is interesting to note what Nehemiah did as a new paradigm leader. I believe that the role of leaders, having set out the broad purpose and put the cells in place, is to establish systems of training, equipping and empowering that will maintain the cells. In a sense, Nehemiah went into the centre and observed. That's what we need to do: go to the centre and look at what is happening. When we see a low bit of the wall, or a weak bit of the wall, we should blow the trumpet and bring help and correction.

This type of leadership is not the absence of leadership; it is just a different style or way of operating. So if the cells are not working well, we need to blow the trumpet and deal with it. If injustice has arisen in our church, again we need to blow the trumpet and deal with it. But the life of the church is on the edges, and we are in the middle, empowering, resourcing and encouraging.

One final question

As we begin to think about whether we want our church to become a cell church, we as the key leaders need to ask ourselves an important question: 'Does our church want to go cell?'

Turning the question around to ourselves, we might ask instead: 'Am I prepared to lead in a new way? Can I as a 30-, 40- or 50-something leader change my style to suit the new dynamic of cell and celebration? Because if I try to take on the idea of cell and all its wonderful complexity, but continue to lead through an old model, I could end up completely disappointed and this thing may never fly.'

Summary

- The leadership style and attitude appropriate to the growth of a cell church is to empower, train and equip others to actually do the work in the cell, the market-place, in evangelism, caring, praying, worshipping and so on.
- Leaders need to encourage the new paradigm of mutual responsibility and empowerment that combats the consumerism within our modern culture.
- Leaders need to fully understand, endorse and encourage the model of cell and celebration.
- Leaders need to be committed to equipping and releasing every member of the church to be involved in ministry, not only the willing few.

- Within the overall vision and purpose of the church, leaders of cell churches need to be encouraged and release every cell and individual to discover for themselves what God would have them do.
- As a model of a leader, Nehemiah was:
  - A man in touch with the heart of God.
  - Prepared to place himself in the purposes of God and be a part of the answer.
  - A man of a vision that was defined and researched.
  - Able to communicate that vision in such a way that the people owned it too, so that they began to work to see the vision realized and cared for each other as they worked.
  - Able to delegate.
  - Able to deal with opposition.

Atmospheres of a Cell Church

Ben Wong (Pastor of the Shepherd Community Church in Hong Kong) has identified ten 'atmospheres' – guiding values – of his church, which he believes are important factors for us all to consider.

We have a positive faith in God

I have come to realize that I can't do it – but God can do it. God is able to do what I cannot do. I am not confined by the possibility of man, but I can do what is possible with God. I am not just a person of the natural but also a person of the supernatural. We all need to operate in the supernatural. If it is hard, then we should do it. If it is easy, then we should not be so thrilled. We can rejoice in our difficulties!

Jesus said in John 16:33 'I have told you these things, so that in me you may have peace. In this world you will have trouble. But take heart! I have overcome the world.'

Some will say, 'Oh, it is so hard', but I believe that we should do it because it is so hard. If I don't think I can do it, then I should do it. If I can do it, then it is too late. When a person does not know how to be a Cell Leader, then they should do it. If they can do it, then they ought to be a Supervisor – otherwise they will stop growing.

I can't do it – so I can depend on God. I do not need to take the burden of the ministry on my own shoulders.

Our church has to be fun!

It is a sin to make church boring. Church ought to be fun. It should be exciting. When we do this, then people will want to bring others to church. We need to distinguish the difference between being serious and being solemn. We can be very serious without being very solemn. In fact, we can be very serious and be very crazy as well! It is possible to have a good sense of humour.

Traditionally, Chinese churches are very solemn, but at my own church we can break out from our old self and be different.

We are constantly bringing out the best in people

We live in a negative society and deal constantly with negative individuals. Any scanning of the news will verify this. In the average Chinese home, negativism prevails. We are prone to be negative people – it is a part of the culture. It is very easy for us to find faults in people – that is no trouble at all. However, to look for the good in others is very foreign to us.

In fact, this is one key reason why so many Hong Kong people have such a low esteem of themselves. Their ability, appearance and intelligence have been ridiculed or questioned repeatedly by their parents, teachers, friends and others in authority. They have been told that they are useless by nearly everyone they have come to respect. The net result is, they see themselves through the negative eyes of others.

A wise Cell Leader will compliment the trait or characteristic he would like to see developed more in those he is leading. It is so very crucial that we train ourselves to be a good finder rather than a fault finder. It is true that all you have to do to find good in a person is to look for it. Every person has good in them. After you have found the good, be sure to do some good by spreading the word. Many times people see the good and then keep it a secret.

Jesus gave us a great example in his treatment of Peter. Before Peter betrayed Jesus three times, he saw that Peter would fail him. However, Jesus saw the best in Peter, not the worst. He saw what Peter could become. He had faith in Peter.

A famous study by Robert Rosenthal, a Harvard psychologist, and Lenore Jacobsen, a San Francisco school principal, furnishes us with a good illustration of this.

A group of primary school pupils was given a test and the next year the new teachers were casually given the names of five or six children in the new class who were designated as 'spurters'; they supposedly had exceptional learning ability. What the teachers did not know was that the test results had been rigged and that the names of these 'spurters' had been chosen entirely at random. At the end of the school year, all the children were re-tested with some astonishing results. The pupils whom the teachers thought had the most potential had actually scored far ahead, and had gained as many as 15 to 27 IQ points. The teachers described these children as happier, more curious, more affectionate than average, and having a better chance of success in later life. But the only change for the year was the change in attitudes of the teachers.

Most of the people who come under our influence will have within themselves a mix of good and bad, strengths and weaknesses. We can choose whether to build on their strengths or become obsessed with their weaknesses. Someone once said, 'There is something that is much more scarce, something finer by far, something rarer than ability. It is the ability to recognize ability.'

Always be on the lookout for hidden capacities!

Sometimes, we as Christians even criticize in our prayers. We are always thinking of the person's problems in order to intercede for them. We concentrate on praying for the person's weaknesses. However, when we read about the apostle Paul praying for people, he gives thanks for them and rejoices over all that the Lord has done. This ought to be our model of praying for others.

The main thing for us is to accomplish the Great Commission

John 4:35 (NIV) 'Do you not say, "Four months more and then the harvest"? I tell you, open your eyes and look at the fields! They are ripe for harvest.'

The field is the world – not the church. We need to change our ecclesiology. The field of our ministry is the world and not in the church. Those of us who are pastors should not call people to come back to church to serve the Lord. We should be in the world to serve the Lord. That is our place of service.

Come to church for two reasons: firstly to be encouraged and healed in order to continue to go out to serve the Lord out there – to continue to fight the war with the evil one. Secondly, come to be equipped in order to know how to fight the fight out there. The purpose of edification is not edification. The reason for edification is the Great Commission.

We are a people with a destiny – we know where we are going

People need to have a vision for their lives. They should know where they are going. They should know that they are destined for a purpose to fulfil and, by the grace of God, they will fulfil that purpose. We are not here by accident. We are all here with a divine purpose.

People should not just wait for things to happen, but rather cause things to happen by actively working out God's will in their lives.

We believe in teamwork and we are good at working together

Our church is committed to teamwork. When we started Shepherd and told a Chinese pastor of our intentions, he told us that he had been ministering in Hong Kong for over 27 years and had never seen a successful team. If we were able to form a successful team, then it would have to be a miracle. We are glad that miracles do happen today.

When one person succeeds, it is because many others want that person to succeed.

Chinese people are famous for not being able to work together. We need to change this fact. We are a new generation of Chinese churches. We are good at unity and we are good at working as a team.

To work together in unity, there must be submission. The leader needs to lead with love; however, the follower needs to follow. Without this, there cannot be teamwork.

We are real people – people of integrity

'Face' is not worth a cent. The key thing is to be real. Integrity is worth everything. We must be on the outside the same as we are on the inside. This is the opposite of being a hypocrite. The Bible says to walk in the light. This means to walk in openness.

Many pastors have fallen into sin in the last few years. Let me ask you, did they suddenly fall into sin by mistake? What really happened? They always had some hidden sins that were not opened up and one day they grew out of proportion and they got found out.

It is all right to fail. All successful people have failed. Failure is the prerequisite to success. All of the great people in the Bible had failures. If leaders can teach people how to handle failure creatively, it may be the most important contribution they can make. Perhaps the one quality that separates the achievers and the masses is the ability to fail.

It is a wise leader who tenaciously teaches people how to learn from their mistakes and not to throw in the towel. It is the wrong notion that to be a good leader, one must not fail. It is foolish for a leader to go to great lengths to hide his failure. We must dispel from our minds the idea that strong people never fail. Strong people make as many and as ghastly mistakes as weak people. The difference is that strong people admit them, laugh at them, learn from them. That is how they become strong.

If you want to convince your group of that, the best way is to let them see you failing. If you try to pretend that it was not a failure, or ignore it, or become more cynical and less of a dreamer for the failure, that lesson, too, will not be lost on them.

It is important that we are constantly changing for the better – change is here to stay

Throughout history, people have resisted change. For 2000 years, people believed that Aristotle was right when he said that the heavier an object, the faster it would fall to earth. He was regarded as the greatest thinker of all times and surely he could not be wrong. 2000 years after Aristotle's death, Galileo summoned learned professors to the base of the Leaning Tower of Pisa. Then he went to the top and pushed off two weights, one weighing ten pounds and the other weighing one pound. Both landed at the same time. But the professors refused to believe and continued to say that Aristotle was right.

God's compassion is new every morning (Lamentations 3:23). God is a God of change. He is the God of the new. God says that the old things will pass away. We have to forget the old and welcome the new. In fact, God says he will bring in the new.

Change is at the centre of the gospel. When a person receives Christ, he is a new creation. The old has passed away. Shepherd is a church of change. We have changed so much since we started seven years ago. People have asked me why Shepherd was able to change so much. My answer is because the people in Shepherd are willing to change.

In our church, there are no spectators – everybody must participate

'It was he who gave some to be apostles, some to be prophets, some to be evangelists, and some to be pastors and teachers, to prepare God's people for works of service, so that the body of Christ may be built up . . . speaking the truth in love, we will in all things grow up into him who is the Head, that is, Christ. From him the whole body, joined and held together by every supporting ligament, grows and builds itself up in love, as each part does its work' (Ephesians 4: 11–16).

God's will for the church is that each person is involved in building up the whole body of Christ. This is a central part of the reformation teaching of Martin Luther – the priesthood of the believers. Everyone is a priest and everyone can serve the Lord.

The church is the community of God's people. It is not a building, nor a programme. It is a people who are living in love for one another and demonstrating to the world the love of God. In a community of love – a cell group – there can be no spectators. Everyone needs to be involved in loving another. This is the church that is designed by Christ.

We are people of the supernatural – God doing the work

'Therefore, if anyone is in Christ, he is a new creation; the old has gone, the new has come!' (2 Corinthians 5:17).

We are a new creation in that when we receive Christ, we are made totally new in the Spirit. Therefore, we are people of the supernatural and not just the natural. We ought to operate not just in the natural, but in the supernatural.

The supernatural is the dimension of God. God is a spirit. The natural is the dimension of the human being. We need to be people who rise up above the human level to God's level. The supernatural is the dimension of faith – the natural is the dimension of sight. We are told not to live by sight but to live by faith. In the supernatural, we can do far more than is humanly possible. It is the dimension where God is working.

This is the dimension that God wants the church to operate in. Let's not limit the church of God by keeping it in the natural, human realm.

City Bands

During the course of the book, I have made mention on a number of occasions of empowering Christians in the market-place and this being a part of the 'every member in ministry' value of the cell church.

In this appendix I have enclosed the outline of an idea we have called City Bands, which is taking one of John Wesley's three structures (Bands) classed as the equivalent of cells and celebrations.

I was asked by a group whether it would be possible for cells to operate in the city and in other market-place towns. My feeling is that for many business people, it would be too hard for them to make the time for a fully functioning cell, particularly in the square mile, but I am sure that's true in Birmingham, Manchester and many other places.

However, 45 minutes where a group of Christians can come together and enpower and encourage one another in their Christian faith and how it relates to the market-place, is more than possible.

City Bands is a simple idea based on cell principles that will enable that to take place.

City Bands: Beliefs

At the heart of City Bands are two beliefs:

1. That when two or three gather together there is Christ in the midst. To demonstrate Christ in the market-place we need to meet with him and experience his presence. There is an added dimension in doing this corporately.
2. That Jesus has called us to a salt and light mandate. All of us are called to be ambassadors for Christ in the market-place by our faith, our words and our actions.

City Bands: Values

City Bands are built on six key values. A personal commitment to each of them is central to the City Band concept.

Jesus at the centre

Taking responsibility for our own relationship with Jesus, and being obedient to him as a lifestyle, is central both to our salvation and to our ongoing walk with God.

Transformation

Personal change is foundational to our faith. We must be committed to change, even when costly or painful. Ours is a God who is concerned for the world. He became flesh and dwelt among us full of grace and truth. As Christians we also have a mandate to change the structures and values around us.

Equipped for the market-place

The ministry of Jesus was to equip his disciples for ministry wherever they were called. We aspire, through the City Bands, to equip one another better to serve him in the market-place. One of our greatest challenges is how we can express, in our working lives, our calling to 'love, joy, peace, patience, kindness, goodness, faithfulness, humility and self-control'.

Outward looking

Our faith is based on relationships as well as the truth, and on a process as well as a decision. May we truly understand this as we discover together how to introduce our colleagues to Christ in a culturally relevant and appropriate way.

Sacrificial love

In a work climate of self-centredness, what greater witness can there be than a life lived for others? City Bands challenge us to express a love that puts others first. Can we love each other and the world with the same passion that Christ has for us?

Honesty

Honesty is the lifeblood of community and is likely to be an essential doorway to growth in a City Band. Without honesty there is no reality, and without reality there is no personal change. It is only as we admit our weaknesses that others can hold us accountable for the future and only as we make ourselves vulnerable that we can find strength in the Lord.

City Bands: Structure

Each City Band meeting has a simple internal structure. This is designed to make it easy for the group to meet and easy for someone to lead. It also helps to keep the group true to the distinct values and beliefs of a City Band.

The structure also enables those considering joining the group to know in advance what is likely to happen and what is expected of them.

City Bands: The three 'P's

Presence

This will be a time for prayer or Bible reading, acknowledging the presence and the power of Jesus in the midst of the group.

Pressure

An opportunity for each person to share a pressure that they are facing personally at work. As the Band members pray for each other the Band will discover more of how Jesus can make a difference to that pressure.

Purpose

Seeking the Lord together for God's heart for the city, for the market-place and for the people who work alongside us. This is so that the reality of God's concern for all aspects of our lives may be realized and our calling to be his ambassadors may be fulfilled.

City Bands: Guidelines

Each Band should ideally be made up of between three and six people who agree to meet either on a weekly or a fortnightly basis for around an hour. Bands can meet before work, at lunch time or in the evening. We have found that relationships develop more quickly if Bands are composed of people who share similar interests.

Each Band should have a facilitator who will organize the venue, help the meeting to flow and keep the Band true to its purpose. The leadership principle should be 'all members in ministry' rather than directional leadership.

Each Band should devote its first few meetings to exploring and understanding the values and beliefs of a City Band. Old habit patterns of small groups may need to be discarded.

Each member should make a commitment to confidentiality.

The Band should commit to meet in accordance with the values and beliefs for, say, six months. It should then review progress.

Moving to Cells

Reproduced here, with permission, is the entire contents of the booklet *Moving to Cells* by Laurence Singlehurst and Liz West.

Cell church beliefs:

- Cell is church.
- Every cell member is in ministry.
- Each cell is a building block of the church (a cell church is only as good as its cells).
- The training and supporting of cell leaders is crucial.

Definition of a cell:

- Church as cell and celebration, with the cell being the building block.
- Every member in ministry; enabling and empowering every single member of the body of Christ.
- Each cell member taking a responsibility to have a network of unchurched friends to whom they are reaching out, and seeking to evangelise and win.

- A sense of mutual accountability to obey the commands of Christ – to love God, love one another, and love the lost.
- Empowering people and encouraging them into a sense of destiny and purpose in what they do on a Monday to Friday basis.

Cell values:

- Jesus at the centre
- Community
- Every member growing
- Every member in ministry
- Evangelism

1. The prototype cell group

Introduction

In seeking to become a cell church, we must keep reminding ourselves that we are in a process that starts where we are right now, and takes us to where we want to go. For the sake of this booklet we will call this the *change process*. This process is concerned with:

- what we believe;
- the values that we take from these beliefs;
- and the structures that serve these beliefs and values.

Having heard something about the cell idea – perhaps read a book, or been to a conference on it – the temptation is to think, 'Yes, I like this,' and jump straight into it. This inevitably means that we violate the change process and end up implementing a new structure. We take our existing small group leaders, we train them in the dynamics of being a cell leader, we try to describe the vision to them, we introduce the idea to the church and we tell them that now all our small groups are cells. I have watched this take place many times and I call it the big bang process.

In one or two churches this method has worked well. But for many others, it has left them with a mixed bag. Some of the trained leaders have understood what is happening and are leading cells. However, many remain as small groups with a new name, and retain a lot of the old weaknesses. Inevitably, some of the leaders, and congregation, feel rushed into the process of becoming a cell church, so when the new vision does not appear to be fulfilling what has been promised, they become disillusioned.

So we want to encourage a slower process which involves two levels of prototype cells, and a period of teaching and preaching to the wider church on the values and visions.

The *Oxford English Dictionary* describes a prototype as 'a trial model, preliminary version'. This trial or preliminary version allows a safe environment to work through and grasp the issues to be faced in the final version. This, of course, applies to any area where a prototype is used – all car manufacturers spend huge amounts of time working with several prototypes before putting their new vehicle on the production line. They know that time invested at the prototype stage saves hours of recall once a model is on sale. The prototype is tested through all the conditions it will face in the real world. It would spell disaster for a car manufacturer to take the designer's drawings and go straight into production.

Our purpose in establishing prototype cells is to train leaders, not just giving them head knowledge, but showing them how to initiate some of the changes in values that need to take place for cell life to become effective. Jesus' strategy was the same; it was focused not on the crowds, but on a small core of leaders. William A. Beckham outlines this in his book *The Second Reformation*:

In John 17 Jesus reported to the Father that their strategy was going to be successful. Why was Jesus optimistic about this? He was facing the cross, the betrayal of Judas and the falling away of the disciples. What was the basis of his confidence? Consider three possible reports Jesus could have presented:

Report Number 1: Our strategy will work because within the first year huge crowds were following Me. I could not get away from them. They clamored for Me to speak to them and even left their homes and jobs to hear Me preach. There was great response and popularity.

Report Number 2: The strategy will work because in the near future, Pentecost will take place. Thousands are going to believe during just one week of time. Therefore, the strategy will work because of the large number of believers who will exist after Pentecost.

Report Number 3: The strategy will work because of the core disciples. These are the ones who have lived with Me in community. I have taught them and lived with them. They know I have come from You, Father! Our strategy will work because of these leaders.

Which report sounds most promising and logical? In light of many traditional church growth methods, Report one or two would appear to have the best chance of success. Both reports have sufficient numbers either at the beginning or the end of the process to forecast expectations of success. However, Jesus confidently gave the third report to the Father. Jesus had a leadership strategy, not a crowd strategy or a numbers strategy . . .

In this leadership context, Jesus related to His leaders in several ways. At times, He related with them one on one, as He did with Peter, Thomas, John, Philip and even Judas. He also related to the Twelve as a unit. Much of His teaching was to the Twelve; He often took them away from the crowds in order to be with them. In a study of the Gospel of Mark, Jim Egli has suggested that 49% of Mark is given to the time Jesus spent with His disciples.

(Chapter 18, 'Jesus' Leadership Strategy')

The first phase of prototype is the leadership team

The main leader of the church gathers together the senior leaders and their spouses (single leaders should be included), and for twelve weeks they experience a prototype cell. This will give them some understanding and experience of what they are getting involved in.

At the end of the prototype, these leaders need to pray and seek God, and ask if this is the way forward for their church. Therefore this is not just the initiative of an enthusiastic leader, since all the senior influencers in the church are going to be involved in approving this new idea.

The second phase of prototype is for potential cell leaders

These are the individuals whom church leaders believe have the necessary skills and character to lead these new cells – which require different skills and abilities to those needed for leading traditional house groups. We call this facilitating leadership. It still requires a level of maturity and leadership, but the leader is going to seek to lead through the people in the cell by a process of facilitation. And the group is as dynamic as the contribution and participation of its members.

These potential cell leaders will, therefore, have experienced what it is like to be in a cell. In the final section of this booklet are suggested cell outlines and the goals to achieve in these two prototypes. These potential cell leaders will – in addition to their twelve weeks in cells – probably need two days of further training. So when they come to lead a cell they will not be leading it purely out of a theory, but out of their own experience.

A note for small churches: in a small church, the people in the leadership prototype may actually be the people who also lead the first cells. This is fine.

2. Goals for prototype cells

Goals for prototype cells

- Gaining a knowledge and understanding of cell values.
- Everyone practised in leading the four 'W's (Welcome, Worship, Word and Witness) taking each section at least twice.
- Feedback given on leadership of the four 'W's section.
- Everyone experiencing edification.
- Understanding the need to create and cast vision.
- Experience the recognised development of small groups through the forming, norming and storming stages.

• Understand the process of relational evangelism through cell.

The above list is not exhaustive, but gives some general goals to work towards in the prototype cells. These goals should be outlined to the group in the early stages and each member's commitment to both the group and the goals should be sought.

A challenge to change our values

One of the goals of the prototype cell group is to challenge the future cell leaders to work together to change their values to those that undergird cell life. In this way they will personally experience edification and can facilitate this in the cells which they will lead in the future. It is crucial that these leaders do not expect others to change if they have not already benefited from the process themselves.

Change begins with honest appraisal of the values that motivate these potential leaders. This honesty comes as a result of the trust that builds within the group. It also requires vision casting – the group needs to see, with the eyes of faith, how an individual and a group of people will look when they are totally motivated out of this biblical value system. They need to see that they can recapture the dynamic of the early church where building a relationship with God, and becoming like Jesus, is their life's calling – kindling a passion for Jesus and a gratitude for what he has done.

The diagram below shows the significant changes that need to happen during the life of a prototype cell.

Understanding the four 'W's

As you will have learned through books and conferences, most cells, within cell churches, have an internal structure. This structure exists to serve the leaders. It is there to ensure that the vision and the values actually happen. And in the future, where we have relatively young Christians (who do not have the maturity and the experience that we have) leading cells, they will be greatly helped by the fact that there is a framework within which to operate.

**Significant changes needed during the life
of a prototype cell**

Value	Change
1. Jesus at the centre	Priority of building relationship with Jesus, and obedience to him as a lifestyle. Knowing God, not only knowing about him.
	Emphasis on hearing from God, resulting in character changing, and fruit of the Spirit growing.
2. Communities of honest relationships marked by sacrificial love	Closer relationships of openness and honesty means more commitment to people, not meetings.
	Resulting conflict, when well managed, is seen to be welcomed as an opportunity for increased wholeness.
	Change of the 'Sunday mindset', whereby church is seen to be the Sunday meeting.
3. Everyone maturing	Expectation that hidden things will come to the surface, and change will happen through the ministry of the whole group.
	Commitment to becoming like Jesus leads to a need for honesty and accountability.
	The result is healing, and freedom from the sin and the pain of the past. Each member becomes a witness with their own story to tell of God's goodness.
4. Everyone using their gifts in ministry	Leaders become facilitators, to enable everyone to make their contribution.
	Each member discovers their gifts, and works to use them to mobilise the body of Christ to work effectively both inside and outside the church.
5. Everyone making God known	Prioritising time to make relationships with people outside the church.
	Working and praying together to create the bridge between Jesus and our friends.
	We have been blessed to be a blessing to others, which is the motivation for outreach.

The beauty of this framework is that it really does help us to experience the vision and the values of the cell. We are then able to train people since we know roughly what is going to happen, whereas in previous house groups there were no clear visions and values, and every group was shaped in the image of its leader.

The four components of a cell meeting are the Welcome, the Worship, the Word and the Witness. As we look at these within the prototype cell, we are in some sense creating a false environment, but because the people involved are leaders, or potential leaders, this is fine. It is an important principle that we don't lead out of head knowledge, and that we don't ask our church members to go where we have not gone. Therefore, in this prototype we want to experience some of the things that they will have to experience, so that their cell leadership training has reality.

The first W is the Welcome   One of the key values within the cell principles is every member in ministry. A second key value is honesty. When the cell meets, the first thing we want to do is to ask everybody an open question, which in our prototype cells we want to make fairly demanding. So we might ask a question such as, 'Where did you hide as a child when life was difficult?' The answers will help us to learn something about each person. Then we might ask, 'Where do you hide as an adult?' Or we could ask, 'What was your coldest physical experience?' Then follow this with, 'What was your coldest emotional experience?' We have included some suggested questions in the prototype cell outlines at the back of this booklet.

What do these questions achieve? First, everyone in that cell has gone from being a spectator to being a participator the moment that each one speaks.

Second, community has begun to form. One of the key ingredients that binds together any group of people is knowing that they have experiences that are common only to them, and that they know things about one another that no one else knows.

I was with a group of leaders where I suggested that we do this. It was met with great disdain. 'But we've known each other for years!' they cried. However, when they went around the room answering the question, 'Which music most influenced you as a teenager?', followed by the question, 'Which person most influenced you, for good or bad?', they learned things about one another that amazed them.

Third, honesty begins to develop, particularly when we go to real cells and the questions are perhaps a little easier at the start. We have to engage in a process where people learn to trust each other with the mundane, because people will probably not share the deep needs of their lives with others until they have learned to trust them with something of little value. We, as leaders, often preach about openness and honesty, but the fact is, we can be some of the most hidden people within our churches. So, both for our main church leaders and our potential cell leaders, this level of honesty is an extremely important part of our prototype experience.

The second W is Worship   Meeting with Jesus and experiencing Jesus, and Jesus being at the centre of our churches and of ourselves, is the major ingredient of the cell vision. It is the major ingredient of church that we love God. When it comes to worship within cells, we want to suggest some perhaps new and creative ways of doing this.

For many groups of this size, worship that is musical can be quite difficult, and may even be embarrassing. Many small groups don't have musicians or people who can really sing. So we want to encourage a mix where, perhaps, there will be some meetings in which we worship with singing as usual, but we also want to explore non-musical worship. For example we might ask the cell members to read John 3:16 and to think, during a couple of minutes' silence, about one thing that strikes them in this verse. Then ask them to share their thoughts. Finally, we could go into a time of open prayer where people give thanks for what they have learned and seen of the nature and wonder of God. In the cell outlines we have included some non-musical worship ideas. This kind of worship actually demands more creativity and participation from the members.

On Sundays we then have the joy of worshipping God through singing and music which, perhaps, we have not used in the cell. But I believe that cell members who have gained confidence through praying and participation in the cell environment would, at a Sunday meeting, be far more bold not only to sing, but also to pray aloud and to take part. It has long been said within leadership circles that one of the greatest challenges is to get the group of leaders to worship. So one challenge of the prototype cell is to get the leaders and the potential leaders to become worshippers and to experience a new dynamic in the presence of Jesus.

The third W is the Word This is perhaps the hardest part to get right, because what we don't want within our cells and prototype cells is a formal Bible study. What we want to experience is more of our values at work. We want an environment for spiritual growth; for every member in ministry; for honesty and accountability. When we multiply the process later on, we will, perhaps, base the word section on what is taught on a Sunday. It may or may not be possible to do this in the prototype process. And again, in the cell outlines, we have made suggestions.

There are three components to the Word section. First, there is something to understand. We want to grapple with the word of God. Second, having understood what was taught on a Sunday, or what we're doing in our prototype, we want to ask, 'What is its application for today?' Go around the group and ask how a particular principle, passage or idea makes an impact on the way we live.

Then we come to the most exciting and difficult part. We ask, 'Who needs help to see this principle or idea at work in their own life?' We very much want to do this in our prototype cells, and hope that this will involve one of the main leaders or one of the potential leaders sharing a need that they have – being honest about a problem or weakness, perhaps even confessing a sin. Then the rest of the group can gather around that individual, maybe sitting them on a chair in the centre, putting an arm on their shoulder, or whatever is appropriate, and every member being encouraged to minister. This can mean several things. Some may pray, others may read an appropriate passage of Scripture. Others might have a gift of the Spirit, a word of knowledge, or a prophecy. We hope to see two things happen: the person receiving prayer meeting with Christ, and the people doing the ministry realising, 'Wow, God can use me!'

But we don't want to leave it there. Cells are not a meeting, they are a community, and the leader of the prototype cell will, where possible, want to encourage practical support among cell members. For example, I was in a cell where a leader and his spouse had their elderly mother living with them. During a cell meeting the leader broke down and shared how hard it was, and how bitter he sometimes felt about having to care for her. He cried out loud to God for a new attitude, and a new heart, and was ministered to and prayed for. The prototype cell leader suggested that the group help him by one or two members giving him a day off from caring for his mother once a week or fortnight so he could get a little respite.

Following this theme, to build community, the prototype cell leader might want to be aware of when a member has a financial need and perhaps take up an offering for it. Or perhaps one of the members has a practical need and the leader wants to encourage the cell members to meet that need. We want to see these things happening in the cells, so we need to experience them in the prototype.

The fourth W is Witness   The cell is here to empower its members into relationships with non-Christians. One goal in the cells is that each cell member will have three local, non-Christian friends and that during a one- to two-year period these friends will have an opportunity to experience Christ through friendship, prayer and the moving of God's Spirit.

Phases of prototype cell development

Now, in our prototype cell we cannot go through an entire cycle. But we want at least to experience some of this in terms of the main church leaders and potential cell leaders having a new passion for the lost. Many of us, as leaders, have very few non-Christian friends. In the cell outlines, we have made some suggestions for you to use in this section.

During the three months of the prototype cell, we want to cover the following areas. First, we want to pray every week and ask God what, within our geographical area, are the main factors that hold people back from giving their lives to Christ. And in each cell we want to spend five to ten minutes praying hard for the area where we live. We trust this will begin to give us a sense of God's heart.

Second, in one or two of the prototype cell meetings, we want to discuss what evangelism is. We aim to come to the understanding that it is a relational process with a non-Christian, and that, through our lifestyle and works, we seek to win them to Christ. This is therefore something in which each of us can be involved. Having discussed that and, we trust, come to a common understanding, we want to address the next stage, which is how we will make local friends. Since we live in a commuting society we often find that the friends we have at work live nowhere near our homes. Because they will not come to our church, we stop living our Christian life in front of them. We must continue to pursue our witness to them, but realise this is a missionary activity as far as their attendance at a local church is concerned.

Third, if we want to see our churches grow, we need to have local friends. How are we going to make these friends? The golden rule is that all friendships are made in the context of something else. In two or three of our cell meetings we want people to get into pairs or triplets and think about which activity they can become involved in within their community so that they make non-Christian friends. For example it might be joining a parent–teacher association or a golf club.

In the witness section of the last of our prototype cell meetings, we will ask people to share how they are going to make non-Christian friends. That is probably as far as we can go within the twelve-week prototype. But we hope both the main leaders and the potential cell leaders will not be asking or challenging their cell members to do something they've not begun to do themselves.

I am sure all of us want to lead meetings that are controlled by the Holy Spirit. It is my firm conviction and experience that having a little structure, such as the one I have outlined, does not limit the Holy Spirit. In some ways it actually helps, because we are creating space for God to break in. And as prototype cell leaders, we want to go into each of these cells having prayed and having called out to God to take our ideas and ask the Holy Spirit to move through them.

Create honesty – help people to share

When it comes to the ministry time, encourage people to reach out expecting a prophecy or a word of knowledge. I believe that we have as a church, within our own nation, often seen God at work in large meetings. We have perhaps seen John Wimber at work, or other people who have a tremendous anointing of the Holy Spirit, but it is my belief and experience that God wants to move as mightily in these small groups of Christians gathering together in cells. And we want to see the Holy Spirit not only moving among us but also among our non-Christian friends in terms of winning them to Christ.

Last of all, we see God building genuine community among us and, we hope, making us groups of Christians who love and care for one another.

The two phases of prototype development

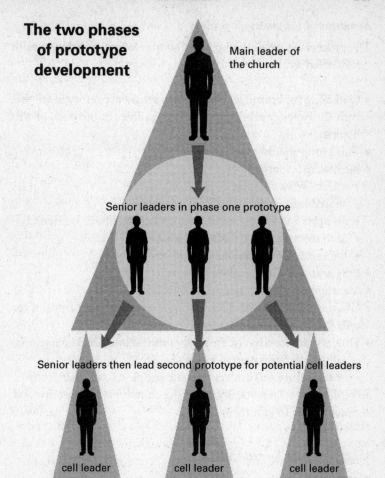

Main leader of the church

Senior leaders in phase one prototype

Senior leaders then lead second prototype for potential cell leaders

cell leader   cell leader   cell leader

Potential cell leaders

Summary of the prototype process

The process we are outlining has a number of stages, which can be summarised as:

- Gathering the central leaders to form an initial prototype cell that runs for twelve weeks, using the cell outlines in the back of this booklet.
- This group should experience:
- facilitative leadership;
  - a four 'W's structure;
  - shared leadership with all participating;
  - an open and honest environment where feedback is given;
  - each member experiencing edification;
  - understanding relational evangelism.
- Pray and seek God to move forward.
- Identify and gather potential cell leaders.
- Use central leadership team to run a second phase of prototype cells with potential cell leaders.
- Multiply the second phase prototypes into the broader church setting:
  - ask people to sign up to join a group;
  - or encourage cell leaders to invite people to join their group.

Note: Do not systematically carve the church list into groups and instruct people to join them!

3. Training steps for cell leaders

During the prototype phase, the future cell leaders experience cell life. It is hoped that they will see that the cell group has brought about growth both for themselves and for the other members. However, they may not have understood why cell life is arranged as it is. This is where the training steps come in. These are useful for all cell leader training and can be used for equipping trainee cell leaders once the cells are up and running.

Having experienced cell life for four to six weeks, it is helpful for the members of the prototype cell to break for a training session. These sessions should be led by the senior church leaders and are most help if they are completed in one day, but they can be broken down into a series of evenings or a half-day. The curriculum should cover:

1. What is a cell church?
   - Vision and values

2. The cell meeting
   - Why the four 'W's?
   - Worship in cell
   - What is edification?

3. The cell cycle
   - Understanding the stages of cell life

As the prototype cell prepares to multiply, further training is useful. At this stage the cell members are preparing to lead a group them- selves, hence the focus of training is on the leadership task.

4. The role of the cell leader
   - What is leadership?
   - Job description
   - Building community
   - Developing a cell vision
   - Facilitating a small group
   - Dealing with different people

After multiplication – probably within the first three months of the new cells – further training is helpful to correspond with the next stage of cell life.

5. How to develop leadership
   - Recognising leadership potential
   - Developing a trainee leader

6. Accountability in the cell
   - How to be a discipler
   - Using the materials from the equipping track
7. Facilitating cell group evangelism
   - Developing a heart motivation
   - Developing a cell strategy

At a later stage:

8. Leading a cell as it multiplies

Resources: *Shepherd's Guidebook* by Ralph Neighbour

4. The next step – multiplying leadership teams

Towards the end of the life of the prototype cell group, the senior leaders should make plans for multiplying those in the cell into leadership teams. There are various options, depending on the size of the church and the readiness of the people to move into cell life.

The first prototype of the leadership team invites potential cell leaders to join in and create second prototype cells, so that all the potential cell leaders have experienced cell life before leading one themselves. There may need to be several second prototype cells so that none exceeds twelve people.

Once the cell leaders have experienced cell life for at least twelve weeks the rest of the congregation can join the cells. Initially these cells should aim to have eight members. This gives new cell leaders an easier job to establish cell life and gives space for growth with new believers. In smaller churches this next phase could include the whole church. The new cell leaders repeat their experience of the prototype cell for the first twelve weeks before branching out to create their own outlines.

For larger churches there will need to be several cell cycles before the whole church is involved. When allocating people to cells it is

helpful to identify potential leaders who can be developed and prepared to take on the next cells after multiplication. These potential
leaders should be placed in cells where there will be a pathway into
leadership after the next multiplication.

Identifying leaders

People leading your existing house groups – where a teaching focus
has been dominant – may not always make the best cell leaders.

The role of the cell leader is crucial to the cell model, so choosing
and developing leaders is a vital task for the church leadership. A
cell leader is a facilitator. This role can be fulfilled by many different
personality types with a variety of gifts.

The following is a helpful checklist when recognising leaders:

The three 'C's

Potential cell leaders should exhibit character, competence and
chemistry.

Character   The cell leader needs to demonstrate godly character. It
is more about who they are than what they do. Godly character can
be described under the HIT principle:

Humility:
Do they know their need of God?
Are they teachable?
Are they willing to serve?
Are they willing to promote others?

Integrity:
Are they willing to be accountable to others?
Do they demonstrate a desire for holiness?
Are they working to overcome sin in their own lives?
Are they working towards being the same on the outside as they are
  on the inside?

Thankfulness:
Do they show a gratitude to God for what he has done for them?
Are they open to God for him to teach them?
Will they be reliant on God in their role as leader?

Competence   If someone is teachable then they can be coached into
the role of leader. The process of developing leaders in cells is in three
parts: experiencing, mentoring and training. The first stage of identifying a leader is to ask them to lead part of a cell meeting. Their reli-
ability and understanding can be evaluated through this. If the culture
in the cell includes positive criticism and feedback, skills can begin to
be developed even before someone is approached to be a cell leader.

The cell leader needs to become skilled at many tasks, including:

• Creating ownership of the cell by all the members.
• Affirming cell members at all times.
• Explaining what is happening, to create security in the group.
• Using body language to encourage contribution.
• Using repetition to emphasise what God has been saying to the group.
• Positive listening, and well-expressed questions.
• Keeping the pace through the meeting.

Chemistry   It is very important for the cell leaders' group to be a
place of safety where leaders can be open, knowing that there is
complete confidentiality and support. If a potential cell leader is
known to be negatively critical of either the model, the vision or the
church leaders themselves, they will destroy the unity in the leadership team. Unless they can be helped through to a place of acceptance and support it is better that they do not become cell leaders,
even if they are gifted.

Establishing cell leaders' meetings

As soon as the prototype cell has multiplied, the church leadership
needs to set in place a support system for the cell leaders. The model

that is generally adopted for this is a monthly cell leaders' meeting plus individual supervision for each leader.

The cell leaders' meetings are the times where:

- the vision for the cell groups is constantly revisited;
- the cell leaders gain support for particular situations;
- issues from the cells can be tackled.

These are usually run by the senior leadership team and regarded as a compulsory part of the job for cell leaders. Trainee cell leaders join this meeting when the multiplication of the cell is expected.

The role of the cell supervisor is to support the cell leader more specifically by meeting with them individually, and also by visiting the cell regularly. They are there to help choose and develop cell leaders, and to help the cell leader through the cell cycle, making sure that the cell is working towards the values behind cell life and not 'swerving to rot' (i.e. missing out one or more of the five cell values). This implies that the cell supervisor is an experienced cell leader, and has, ideally, led a cell group through every stage of cell life to multiplication, including leading someone to the Lord, and developing the next leaders. Initially this role needs to be taken by the church leaders who will be the most experienced cell leaders, having led the prototype cell. It is difficult to lead a cell group and also supervise another one. It is also difficult to supervise more than three cells at any one time.

5. Using the cell outlines in your prototypes

There are twelve cell outlines for you to use as you run both the first- and second-stage prototype cells. These cover the five core values of cell church and are ordered to give a natural development in value change as they are used.

The value to be covered is at the top of each page, followed by the four 'W's sections. As a guide, the welcome should take 20 minutes, worship 20 minutes, word 40 minutes and witness 20 minutes. You will find that the timing of these sections varies enormously, and in the initial stages it will be important to spend an extended time with the ice-breaker.

Remember, as you give the various sections to members of your group, it is important to give feedback on how they have done. You may want to phone them the following day or have a brief conversation with them before you depart.

Value

Jesus at the centre.

Welcome

Tell the group three things about yourself which they do not already know, one of which is untrue. Ask the group to guess which one you have made up.

Worship

Go around the group asking each person to say something about the character of God which they appreciate, and why it is particularly relevant at this time. Lead a time of thanking God for these aspects of his character.

Word

Goal: to highlight our motivation for the choices we make. If Jesus comes first in our lives our motivation to be obedient will show in the choices we make. Ask the group to think of some significant choices they have made recently. Share some of these with the group, describing briefly the process of their decision-making. Ask whom they were motivated to please in the decisions they made.

Read John 14:15. Jesus wants us to be motivated out of love for him.

Ask the group to list some reasons why we should be obedient to Jesus. (For example Romans 5:6–8: God's love for us demonstrated in Jesus' death; Deuteronomy 5:33: obedience results in blessing.)

In pairs or triplets, share one area where you are struggling to be
obedient to God and then pray for each other. Or, pray for specific
choices that are imminent, that these choices will be motivated out
of obedience.

Witness

In the same way that we want Jesus at the centre of our own lives,
we also want him to be Lord over the area where we live. As a group,
identify the strongholds that are standing against Jesus' rule in your
area, e.g. materialism, 'religion', pride, educational achievement.
Pray together for these to be broken.

Value

Cells are communities where there is sacrificial love within open and honest relationships.

Welcome

Name one thing that makes you feel loved. Name one thing that makes you feel unloved.

Worship

Remember the things God has done which show that he loves you – share these with the group. Either thank him for these things, or worship him by singing or playing a chorus with the theme of thanking God for his love for us.

Word

Read 1 John 3:16–24.
Make a list of the things these verses tell us to do.

Ask the group to list the times when they can remember these things being done in the church.

What does it mean to 'lay down our lives for our brothers'?

Spend some quiet time seeing if 'our hearts condemn us' (verse 20).

As a group, or in pairs, confess aloud the things that come to your mind, ask God for forgiveness if necessary and be accountable to each other in trying to change. Pray for each other, asking God to help you to do these things.

Witness

Read John 13:35.
Jesus says that our especially loving community will have an impact on unbelievers.

   If God is asking us to be marked by our love for one another, how can we achieve this in the cell?

Value

Every member in ministry.

Welcome

Say which colour describes the kind of day you have had, and why.

Worship

Choose a song from a worship CD or tape. Ask God to speak to you through the music. Listen to the track and then ask the group to write down what it makes them think about. Share these things in the group.

Word

Read 1 Corinthians 12:1–12 and 27–31.

Which gifts are listed in verses 7–10? Make a list on a flip chart or large sheet of paper. Check understanding by asking different people to describe each gift, giving an example of when they have seen the gift in action. Add a definition of each gift to your flip-chart list.

Discuss together what happens to the whole church if each gift is missing. Add your answers to the list.

We are told to 'eagerly desire the greater gifts'. To your list of the gifts add the name of each cell member who would like to have that gift or to grow in using it. Ask God to help you by praying for each other to receive this gift and to have the boldness to use it.

Work out specific ways that you can hold each other accountable to use these gifts in the context of the cell group. Remember: return to your list often to make sure everyone is growing in using the spiritual gifts.

Witness

The cell has looked at ways of developing a loving community. How can you expose non-believers to this special community? (John 13:35.)

Plan a specific event where you can do this. Pray for God to bless your plans.

Value

Every member maturing.

Welcome

What is your greatest challenge in terms of spiritual growth?

Worship

If you have a musician in the group, ask them to prepare and lead about ten minutes of worship choruses. If no musician is available, ask a group member to bring a CD or tape and lead the group in a time of worship, either by singing with the track or by meditating on the words as they are sung. You may need to write out the words and have a copy for each person.

Word

Read Philippians 3:12–14 and 1 Corinthians 9:24–27.
The Christian life is like a journey or a race. From 2 Corinthians 17–18 what is one goal of this journey? (To be like Jesus.)

Ask someone else to **read Hebrews 12:1–13**. What holds us up on the journey? What kind of things does Paul mean by 'everything that hinders and the sin that so easily entangles'?

In pairs or triplets, ask each other for honest answers to the question: 'What things are stopping me from becoming more like Jesus?' There are many answers, but it could be a specific recurring sin or hurt from the past, unbelief or lack of faith.

Pray for each other, asking God for a breakthrough in these areas. You could use Romans 8:1–3 as encouragement.

Ask cell members to be accountable to each other about the things they have shared, and to encourage one another to change.

Witness

Spend some time praying again for God to establish his kingdom in your neighbourhood.

WEEK 5

Value

Everyone making God known.

Welcome

How did you become a Christian?

Worship

Read Psalm 121 together. Divide the Psalm into four sections of two verses each. Give these sections to cell members and ask them to write a thanksgiving prayer about their section. Read the Psalm again, stopping after each section so that the prayers can be read out after the relevant verses.

Word

What does Jesus think and feel about the lost? **Read Luke 15:1–7** (you could continue in Luke 15 to read the parable of the lost coin and the lost son).

What example does Jesus set us?

Do you feel the same as Jesus does about your friends who do not know him? Ask for honest answers and then pray together to receive God's heart for the lost.

Witness

The group needs to build a cell list of non-Christian friends to pray for to become Christians. Ask each member to name three people who live locally and who are not Christians. This needs to be done prayerfully in order to choose those whom they believe God is asking them to build a relationship with. For some cell members this might mean beginning new relationships with neighbours or taking up a new interest in order to make contacts. It is important to be real about where cell members are on this – for some it means a lifestyle change to make time for these friendships.

WEEK 6

Value

Everyone making God known.

Welcome

Who influenced you most when you were twelve years old?
Who influences you most now?

Worship

In a time of silence, ask the group to come before God in repentance, confessing wrong attitudes and evidence of selfishness in their lives. You could choose to focus on repentance around attitudes to the lost.

Worship God together by thanking him for his accepting love and forgiveness.

Word

Read Luke 10:5–12.

Ask the group to work out Jesus' strategy for evangelism. It should look something like this:

Pray; **go** and make relationships; **find** those who are men and women of 'peace'; **build** relationships with them; **wait** for, or create, an opportunity to pray with them for a felt need; when they are ready, tell them about the 'good news'.

Jesus lived in a world much like our own postmodern culture. Ask the group to work out how this strategy applies to their situation.

What is the next step for them individually, and as a group, to see friends come to know Jesus?

Witness

Work out the next step for those in your network of friends on the 'cell list'. Is it to deepen those friendships or have the courage to pray with your friends, to believe God will answer prayers, or to know how to 'tell them'? Pray for opportunities and God's blessing as you reach out to these friends.

Remember to ask about answers to these prayers next week.

WEEK 7

Value

Biblical communities are marked by honesty.

Welcome

What would stop you from being honest?

Worship

Encourage the group to be a thankful people by sharing things that have made them grateful to God.

Ask everyone to thank God for these specific things that he has done for them.

Word

What can we learn about how we should relate to one another?

Read the following verses to find some of the answers: **1 Thessalonians 3:12; Ephesians 4:15–16; Hebrews 10:24–25; James 5:16.**

Discuss what helps the development of trust and honesty. Which things stand against us being open?

Name specific ways in which we need to work harder at being open with one another. Be accountable to each other in this.

Pray for members whose past experiences have made them wary of trusting others.

Witness

Ask the cell members how they are progressing with their friendships. Pray again for those on the cell list, that they will become open to the gospel.

WEEK 8

Value

Jesus at the centre.

Welcome

How does God communicate with you? Give an example from your own life.

Worship

Read Psalm 23.

Think of times when the truth in this Psalm has been evident in your life. Give God the glory for the great things he has done. Find your own way to do this, or write a poem or psalm together, or sing praises to him.

Word

Read John 10:1–6.

What conditions have to be in place for us to hear God's voice? Make a list from these verses and from the experiences of the group. Encourage people to share their experiences of hearing from God.

If we are going to effectively use our gifts to minister within the cell, and to those outside the church, we need to grow in confidence about hearing from God. Ask each cell member what they think is the next step for them, then pray for each other to move forward in this.

Ask someone to share a current situation where they need to hear from God. Lead the group in a time of listening to God about this situation. Believe that he is going to speak and go around the group afterwards to hear what they believe he said. (This can be a contrived situation, but God is very gracious and wants to encourage us in listening to him, so do not underestimate what might happen.)

Witness

In pairs, ask God what is stopping each one's three friends on the cell list from becoming Christians. Expect God to reveal an area of wrong thinking, sin or something in their circumstances. When you have heard for each person, pray into their situation.

Value

Jesus at the centre.

Welcome

What stimulates your walk with God?

Word

The purpose of this week is to encourage everyone to be worshippers. Read the story of the woman at the well from **John 4**. What can we learn about worship from this passage?

1. Knowing whom we worship.
   In what areas do I need to grow and expand my understanding of who God is?
2. Not where we worship, but how.
   Read Psalm 24:3–4.
   What do we need to worship?
   Are there any aspects of my life which are a barrier to me coming close to God? **Read Romans 8:15–16.**
3. Real worship is spiritual.
   Ask God to fill us with his Holy Spirit.

Worship

Lead an extended time of worship, either by singing or with a CD or tape of worship songs. You could begin this with a time of confession and lead into intimate expression of gratitude to God for who he is and what he has done.

Witness

Do you know how to tell people the truth about Jesus?

    Read John 8:44.

    How does Jesus describe the enemy in this verse?

    What would 'doing the opposite' involve?

    What equipping do you think you need to be able to explain the gospel to one of your friends? Pray, and plan to address the issues that come up.

Value

Community – what is love?

Welcome

If you could change one thing about yourself what would it be?

Worship

Open with a time of confession, asking the Holy Spirit to bring to mind anything we need to confess, thinking especially of anything we have done that has been unloving, e.g. gossip, using people, lusting, not doing something for someone and so on.

Thank God that he forgives us.

Word

What do you do when you've been hurt? Broken relationships need attention.

Read Matthew 6:14–15 and Colossians 3:12–14.

From these verses what is the key to mending broken relationships?

Who can give an account of when they forgave someone, and what happened as a result?

Is there anyone in the cell who needs to ask for forgiveness from another cell member, or who needs to forgive someone?

Is anyone struggling to forgive someone right now?

Pray for each other.

Witness

Do you have any difficulties in your relationships with any of your unbelieving friends or family? Is there anyone you need to forgive? Is there anyone you need to ask forgiveness from? How can you put this relationship right? What's the next step?

Pray for one another and next week remember to ask how it went.

Value

Every member in ministry.

Welcome

What was the best present you ever received? What made it especially important?

Worship

Build a pile of Ebenezer stones. Bring several stones to the group,
enough for each person to have three or four.

    Read 1 Samuel 7:12 and together make a list of the times God has
given generously to you as a group or as individuals. Each time you
remember an occasion when the Lord has helped you, place a stone
on the pile in the centre of the room.

Word

Read Romans 12:1–8.

List the eight motivational gifts, explaining that a motivational gift
is something that affects our behaviour, creating a tendency for us
to behave in a certain way in many different situations.

    Everyone will tend towards one or maybe two main motivational
gifts. The goal of this time is for each person to begin to recognise
their gift. Work as a group, or in pairs, to create a definition of each
gift. Share these definitions. Then ask the pairs to help each other
remember times when they have felt pleased or found satisfaction
with what they have done, or when they have been complimented by

others. From these memories ask them to work towards knowing their gift. Suggest they continue to think and pray about this during the week and leave a time to share their conclusions at the next cell meeting.

Witness

Use this time to plan another social event when you can meet with each other's friends from the cell list. Ask God to show you what to do and for him to bless your plans.

Value

Every member in ministry.

Welcome

What do you think is your motivational gift from the list in Romans 12? Give reasons why you have chosen this gift.

Worship

As a more active time of worship, ask the group to think of attributes of God's character and write each of them on a sheet of A4 paper. You will need to name more attributes than there are people in the group. Place the papers randomly on the floor. Cell members then move around the room standing on a piece of paper and all together praise God aloud for the character attribute they are standing on. They move on to the next piece of paper when they are ready and again praise God aloud.

Word

Read John 7:37–39 and Luke 11:11–13.
What did Jesus teach about the Holy Spirit from these two passages?

From **Romans 8:5–11**, why do we need the Holy Spirit in order to be effective in ministry?

Get the group to check their motives for wanting to be filled with the Holy Spirit, by challenging them to confess unbelief or disobedience and then pray for one another to be filled with the Holy Spirit.

Witness

Now that you know more about the gifts God has given you, how can you use these gifts to bless your non-Christian friends and family? Work in pairs, preferably with those who have the same gift, to answer this question. Pray for each other to have opportunity, creativity and courage to use your gifts in evangelism.

Ask the group to continue to pray and think through this question and to bring their conclusions to the next cell meeting.

Resources

Introductory reading

Body and Cell	Howard Astin
Home Cell Group Explosion	J. Comiskey
House To House	Larry Kreider
Radical Renewal	H. Snyder
Second Reformation	Bill Beckham
Sowing Reaping Keeping	Laurence Singlehurst
Where Do We Go From Here?	Ralph Neighbour
Epidemic Of Life	Chris Thackeray
Apostolic Cell Church	Lawrence Khong
Moving To Cells	Laurence Singlehurst
Reap The Harvest	Joel Comiskey
Heirs Together	Daphne Kirk
Shouting In The Temple	Lorna Jenkins

Leaders' reading

The Shepherd's Guidebook	Ralph Neighbour
Heirs Together	Daphne Kirk

Groups Of Twelve	Joel Comiskey
Leadership Explosion	Joel Comiskey
Red Hot Icebreakers	M. Puffett and S. Rottler
The Cry for Spiritual Fathers and Mothers	Larry Kreider
Encounter God Manual	Jim Egli
Encounter God Instructor's Guide	Jim Egli
Encounter God Retreat Guide	Jim Egli
Healing Souls Touching Hearts	Dr G. Sweeten and S. Griebling
What Shall We Do With The Children?	Daphne Kirk

Ralph Neighbour Equipping Track

Dr Ralph Neighbour is a pioneer of the cell church movement and his books are foundational works.

Welcome To Your Changed Life	Ralph Neighbour
New Believer's Station	Ralph Neighbour
Your Journey Guide	Ralph Neighbour
The Arrival Kit (UK version)	Ralph Neighbour
Sponsor's Guidebook	Ralph Neighbour

Lawrence Khong Equipping Track

Lawrence Khong is the pastor of Faith Community Baptist Church in Singapore, which is a leading cell church of 10,000 people.

Welcome To Your New Life	Lawrence Khong
Your New Journey Guide	Lawrence Khong
Beginning Your New Life	Lawrence Khong
Living Your New Life	Lawrence Khong

Youth Cell Equipping Track

Cell It (Youth Manual)	Liz West
Youth Cell Leader's Handbook	Sublime
James, Peter and John	Sublime
Passion	Paul Hopkins

Children's Cells Equipping Track

Living With Jesus	Daphne Kirk
Hand In Hand	Daphne Kirk
Family Journeys Together	Lorna Jenkins
Living Life Upside Down	Lorna Jenkins
Now I Follow Jesus	Lorna Jenkins

Further reading

Nine Ways To Effective Group Leading	Carl George
Cell Leader Guidebook	Ralph Neighbour
Cell Leader Trainer's Guide	Ralph Neighbour
Celling The Church Kit	Paul Weaver
Cover The Bible	Ralph Neighbour
Helping You Build Cell Churches	L. Kreider and B. Sauder
How To Read The Bible	Lawrence Khong
Icebreakers	Randall Neighbour
Leading Children's Cell Groups	Lorna Jenkins
Children's Journey Guide	Lorna Jenkins
When A Child Asks To Be Baptised	Daphne Kirk
Touching Hearts	Ralph Neighbour
Biblical Foundation Series (12 books)	Larry Kreider

Materials for healing weekends

Encounter God	Jim Egli
Search for Significance	Robert S. McGee
Steps to Freedom in Christ	Neil Anderson

Healing for the Nations run retreats for groups. They can be contacted at 24 Scotforth Road, Lancaster LA1 4ST.

The books listed above can be ordered from the YWAM bookshop on 02476 348128 or email bookshop.kl@ywam.org.uk

Please don't forget to visit the Cell UK web site at www.cellchurch.co.uk

This web site links up with major cell web sites around the world and contains lists of icebreakers, worship activities, and many helpful articles.

Finally, we would like to mention *Cell Church UK* – a magazine to help you discover what's happening in cells throughout the UK and worldwide. It is currently published four times a year at a cost of £12.00 (UK) or £15 overseas. Contact Cell UK at Highfield Oval, Harpenden AL5 4BX or email celluk@oval.com